WHY?

by Donnie V. Rader

ONE STONE
BIBLICAL RESOURCES

Published by:
One Stone Press
979 Lovers Lane
Bowling Green, KY 42103

Printed in the United States of America

ISBN 10: 0-9854938-5-2
ISBN 13: 978-0-9854938-5-1

Supplemental Materials Available:
PowerPoint slides for each lesson
Answer key
Downloadable PDF

www.onestone.com

Preface

Peter wrote, "But sanctify the Lord God in your hearts, and always be ready to give a defense to everyone who asks you a reason for the hope that is in you, with meekness and fear" (1 Peter 3:15). The word for "defense" ("answer" KJV) is the word *apologian* (apology). It means to give a defense, answer or reason for what we believe.

Truth has a defense to questions that are asked. Truth has answers to challenges it faces. We, as God's people, need to know why we believe what we believe and why we practice what we practice. We need to prepare ourselves to answer the questions of why we believe and practice what we do.

The following lessons are an attempt to help us answer such questions.

Table of Contents

WHY WE BELIEVE
It Makes A Difference What One Believes

A very popular concept is it makes no difference what one believes in religion. We hear our religious friends say things like, "Faith alone will save, just believe in the Lord." Many say, "Sincerity is all that matters." Thus, it makes no difference what one believes, we are told. We are encouraged to "Join the church of your choice." After all, "One faith is as good as another," it is thought. Good moral people are sometimes equated with being Christians (no matter what their belief or practice is religiously). All of this says that most of our religious friends think it really doesn't matter what one believes in religion.

This concept is one of the greatest obstacle to teaching others the gospel. When we invite someone who believes it makes no difference what one believes, he or she will not be really interested in going to services with us. When we try to set up a Bible study with our friends, they likely will decline, because, to them, it makes no difference.

If it does not make any difference what one believes, there is no need to study the questions and issues that divide the religious world. Those issues become trivial matters. Questions about baptism, the Godhead, the one church, worship, instrumental music, the operation of the Holy Spirit and the work and organization of the church are all like the question of where Cain got his wife. In spite of their lack of understanding, those who are deceived by this concept are made to feel comfortable no matter what they believe or practice. Since it does not make any difference, why should different beliefs and practices concern them?

If those who think this way already have a church they go to, they do not need another. Thus, when you invite them to visit with you or attend a gospel meeting, they may politely thank you, saying they already go to _____ church. Since "one church is as good as another," they need another church about like a man with a new car needs another car.

This concept is one of the devil's most effective tools. As long as one has the concept that it does not make any difference what one believes, the gospel cannot get through that barrier to penetrate the heart.

As long as one has the concept that it **does not make any difference** what one believes, the gospel cannot **get through that barrier** to penetrate the heart.

Several reasons can be given as to why we believe it makes a difference what one believes.

There is an objective standard.

1. **Objective versus subjective standards**. A subjective standard varies from person to person. When someone appeals to what "I think" or how "I feel" or what their family believes or did, that is using a subjective standard. The same is true when using their preacher or what some book of men says.

   An objective standard is fixed; it is the same for all.

2. **The Bible, the word of God, is the objective standard we have in religion**. All of the following are descriptions of that standard. We must abide by what is written of God (2 Cor. 4:13), the oracles of God (1 Pet. 4:11), the commandments of the Lord (1 Cor. 14:37), the word of God (1 Thess. 2:13), the inspired Scriptures (2 Tim. 3:16-17), and the words chosen by the Holy Spirit (1 Cor. 2:9-13).

   If there is an objective (fixed) standard, then it makes a difference what one believes. The principle also works in reverse. If it makes a difference what one believes, then there must be an objective standard we have to follow.

   Let's consider a parallel. Suppose that you are building a new house and a friend offers to do the wiring for free. You wonder if it really makes any difference how you wire the house. Suppose the standard he wants to use is what he thinks, how he feels, or what some electrician told him. Or what if he said he would wire it like his dad wired his house or like a neighbor had done his? In all of this he is using a **subjective** standard (for it varies from person to person). When you discover that there is a National Electric Code (an **objective** standard) you understand that it makes a difference how one wires the house.

There is one faith.

1. **The Bible speaks of "one faith," not "faiths."** Paul wrote, "There is one body and one Spirit, just as you were called in one hope of your calling; one Lord, **one faith**, one baptism; one God and Father of all, who is above all, and through all, and in you all" (Eph. 4:4-6; emphasis mine, DVR).

2. **"One faith" means "only one faith."** When the same text says "one Spirit" (v. 4), does that mean only one Spirit or that there could be many spirits? When the same text says "one Lord" (v. 5), does that mean only one Lord or that there could be many Lords? When it says there is "one God" (v. 6),

> If it makes a difference what one believes, then there must be an **objective standard** we have to follow.

does that mean that there is only one God, or that there could be many Gods? The conclusion we draw about each of these must be the same with "one faith".

3. **There is no such thing as "my faith," "your faith," or "different faiths."**

It is possible to believe a lie and be lost.

1. **The young prophet believed a lie and was punished (1 Kings 13).** God gave him three simple rules. They were, "You shall not eat bread, nor drink water, nor return by the same way you came" (v. 9). He clearly understood, for he explained it to the king (v. 9) and to the old prophet who followed after him (vv. 16-17). However, the old prophet said that God had told him to "bring him back to your house, that he may eat bread and drink water" (v. 18). Then the text says, "but he lied to him" (v. 18). We know this was a lie for two reasons. First, the text says it was (v. 18). Second, this was the exact opposite of the truth.

   Did it make any difference which of these he believed and followed? He believed the old prophet's lie and went back with him, ate bread and drank water (v. 19). Because he was disobedient, God caused a lion to kill him (vv. 20-34).

2. **Those who believe a lie will perish (2 Thess. 2:10-12).** Note the contrast in this passage between those who believe a lie and those who believe the truth. Those who believe the truth (v. 12) and love the truth (v. 10) will be saved (v. 10). However, those who are deceived (v. 10), deluded (v. 11) and believe a lie (v. 11) will perish (v. 10) and be condemned (v. 12). Thus, it makes a difference what one believes.

One can be religious and be wrong.

1. **Cain's offering was not accepted (Gen.4:3-5).** The text says, "And in the process of time it came to pass that Cain brought an offering of the fruit of the ground to the Lord. Abel also brought of the firstborn of his flock and of their fat. And the Lord respected Abel and his offering, but He did not respect Cain and his offering. And Cain was very angry, and his countenance fell" (Gen. 4:3-5).

   Both Cain and Abel brought an offering before God. Cain brought from the fruit of the ground. Abel gave from the firstborn of his flock. They both were religious. They both were attempting to worship God. Yet, the Lord respected Abel's sacrifice but did not respect Cain's. What was the difference? The Hebrew writer said, "By faith Abel offered to God a more excellent sacrifice than Cain, through which he

If one can be **religious** and be **wrong**, then it makes a difference **what** one believes in religion.

obtained witness that he was righteous…" (Heb. 11:4). Abel's offering was by faith, thus Cain's was not. Since faith comes by the word of God (Rom. 10:17), we conclude that Abel's offering was according to God's word and Cain's was not.

2. **Nadab and Abihu's sacrifice did not please God (Lev. 10:1-2).** The text says, "Then Nadab and Abihu, the sons of Aaron, each took his censer and put fire in it, put incense on it, and offered profane fire before the LORD, which He had not commanded them. So fire went out from the LORD and devoured them, and they died before the LORD" (Lev. 10:1-2).

Though they were religious, and attempted to serve God, their sacrifice was not accepted. They offered profane fire ("unauthorized fire" NIV) which God had not commanded. Thus, God caused a fire to devour them.

If one can be religious and be wrong, then it makes a difference what one believes in religion.

Absurd consequences

We believe it makes a difference what one believes in religion because of the absurd consequences of thinking otherwise. If it makes no difference what one believes, then the following is true.

1. **Directly opposite doctrines and practices are equal.** That would mean that the doctrine that says Jesus is the Son of God and the doctrine that says he is not the Son of God would be equal. This would mean the doctrine that says a Christian can fall from grace and the doctrine that says once saved always saved are equal. The same is true with every doctrine that contradicts another doctrine.

2. **We can do anything we want in religion.** If we can't, then it must make a difference what one believes and practices. But, if it doesn't make any difference what one believes and practices, then we can do absolutely anything we want to do.

3. **It doesn't matter whether one believes or not.** If it doesn't make any difference what we believe, it doesn't matter whether we believe at all! If someone says, "Oh no, you have to believe in God, in Christ and in the Bible," then it makes a difference.

4. **It doesn't make any difference whether one believes the Bible.** To say it makes no difference what one believes, is saying one doesn't have to believe the Bible. If that is true, what the Bible says is unimportant. That would mean what God says is unimportant! That is simply blasphemy!

> If it doesn't make any difference what one **believes and practices**, then we can do **absolutely anything** we want to do.

Conclusion

For these reasons (and perhaps many others) we conclude it makes a difference what one believes. Since that is true, we need to know the truth (John 8:32). Since this is true, we need to study and examine what we are taught (Acts 17:11). Since this is the case, we need to prepare ourselves to tell others "why we…" (1 Pet. 3:15).

Questions

1. How does this popular concept (that it makes no difference what one believes) create an obstacle to teaching others the gospel? _____
    _____
    _____
    _____

2. What is the difference in an objective and subjective standard? _____
    _____
    _____

3. Can you think of other parallels (besides wiring a house) that illustrate how an objective standard has to be used? _____
    _____
    _____
    _____

4. How can we show that "one faith" means only one faith? _____
    _____
    _____
    _____

5. What was the truth that the young prophet (1 Kings 13) was told to follow? _____
    _____
    _____

6. What was the lie the old prophet told the young prophet (1 Kings 13)? _____
    _____
    _____

7. How does 2 Thessalonians 2:10-12 show that it makes a difference? _____
    _____
    _____

8. What was the difference in Cain's offering and Abel's offering? _____
    _____
    _____

9. What was wrong with the offering Nadab and Abihu gave? _____
    _____
    _____

10. What kind of consequences can be attached to the view that says it does not make a
    difference what one believes? _____
    _____
    _____

11. Can you list some other consequences besides those that are given in this lesson? _____
    _____
    _____
    _____
    _____

WHY WE BELIEVE
Baptism Is Essential for Salvation

The essentiality of baptism has been disputed by many in the religious world. Some teach that one is saved by faith before and without water baptism. The Bible teaches that one must be baptized in water to be saved. Consequently, there have been many religious debates on the question. Many of our friends believe in baptism and practice it, but do not believe it to be essential to salvation.

The question

In any controversy it is helpful to clarify what the issue really is.

1. **What the question/issue is not**. The question at hand is not whether or not one is saved by faith. We are. It is not whether or not one is saved by the blood of Christ. We are. It is not whether or not one is saved by God's grace. We are. It is not whether or not we are saved by baptism alone. We are not. It is not a question of whether we are saved by works of merit. We are not. Neither is it a question of whether one is saved by water. We are not.

2. **What the question/issue is**. The question is whether or not water baptism is essential to salvation. It is *when* or *at what point* one is saved by faith. It is a question of *when* or *at what point* the blood of Christ is applied.

3. **Why is this so important?** If baptism is essential, then any who are not baptized will be lost. And, those that teach it is not essential are false teachers. However, if it is not essential, then those who teach that it is are binding where God has not bound.

The evidence

1. **Mark 16:16 – Essential to be saved**. The text says, "He that believeth and is baptized shall be saved; but he that believeth not shall be damned." Let's consider two opposite statements. First, "He that believes and is baptized shall be saved." Second, "He that believes is saved, and then he

> If baptism is **essential**, then any who are not baptized will be **lost**. And, those that teach it is not essential are **false teachers**.

should be baptized." Which one of those do you believe? Which one of those is what Jesus said?

Here is a sentence that is parallel in structure. "He that eats and digests shall be healthy, but he that does not eat shall be unhealthy." What is essential to eating? You understand, it is eating and digesting. However, to be unhealthy all I have to do is leave off eating. Likewise, this passage says there are two things essential to be saved.

Let's suppose Ford Motor Company said, "He that believeth in Ford Motor Company and is baptized in our pool shall receive a new Ford." What must one do to get the new Ford? Could one argue, "I believe, so give me the Ford and then I will be baptized"?

2. **Acts 2:38 – For the remission of sins**. The text says, "Then Peter said unto them, Repent, and be baptized every one of you in the name of Jesus Christ for the remission of sins, and ye shall receive the gift of the Holy Ghost." Note that repentance and baptism are joined by the coordinating conjunction "and." They are joined like two railroad cars. The direction in which one of those goes, so goes the other. If repentance is "for" (in order to obtain) the remission of sins, so is baptism. However, if baptism is "for" (because of; that is, one has already received) the remission of sins (as some argue), then repentance goes in the same direction.

> If baptism is because sins have **already** been forgiven, then Jesus shed his blood for the **same reason**.

A parallel passage where "for the remission of sins" is found will help us understand its meaning. Jesus shed his blood "for the remission of sins" (Matt. 26:28). That is the same expression (in English and Greek) as found in Acts 2:38. If baptism is because sins have already been forgiven, then Jesus shed his blood for the same reason. Yet, if the blood was shed in order to obtain the remission of sins, then we are baptized for the same reason.

3. **1 Peter 3:21 – Saves us**. The text says, "The like figure whereunto even baptism doth also now save us (not the putting away of the filth of the flesh, but the answer of a good conscience toward God) by the resurrection of Jesus Christ." Let's again consider two opposing statements. First, "Baptism doth NOW save us." Second, "Baptism doth NOT save us." Which one of those do you believe? Which one of those is what Peter said?

Notice the comparison in the context. Eight souls (Noah and his family) were transported from the old world (before the flood) to the new world (after the flood) by means of water. Thus, the eight souls were saved by water. Likewise ("the like figure"), we are transported from our old life of sin to a new life of salvation by baptism.

4. **Galatians 3:26-27 – Baptized into Christ.** The text says, "For ye are all the children of God by faith in Christ Jesus. For as many of you as have been baptized into Christ have put on Christ." Paul affirms "you are" something. What are they? They are the children of God by faith (v. 26). Then, he says "For" (denoting the reason which follows). The reason is "You have been" baptized into Christ. The point is, these were the children of God because they had been baptized.

5. **In every case of conversion, the person was baptized.** Not every case specifically mentions faith, but we know from other passages that faith is essential. Not every case specifically mentions repentance, but we know that repentance is essential because of other passages. Yet, every case mentions baptism.

> In **every case** of conversion, the person was **baptized**.

Cases of Conversion					
Case	**Hear**	**Believe**	**Repent**	**Confess**	**Baptism**
Jews	Acts 2:22	Acts 2:36	Acts 2:38		Acts 2:38
Samaritans	Acts 8:5	Acts 8:12			Acts 8:12ff
Eunuch	Acts 8:35	Acts 8:36-37		Acts 8:37	Acts 8:38
Saul	Acts 9:6				Acts 22:16
Cornelius	Acts 11:14	Acts 10:43	Acts 11:15		Acts 10:48
Lydia	Acts 16:14				Acts 16:15
Jailor	Acts 16:31	Acts 16:31	Acts 16:33		Acts 16:33
Corinthians	Acts 18:8	Acts 18:8			Acts 18:8

6. **Salvation is in Christ – We are baptized into Christ.** Paul wrote, "In whom we have redemption through his blood…" (Eph. 1:7). What is taking place? Redemption. Where does it take place? In Him (Christ). How does it take place? By the blood. In the next chapter he wrote, "But now in Christ Jesus ye who sometimes were far off are made nigh by the blood of Christ" (Eph. 2:13). Again, what is being discussed? Being made near means the same as redemption. Where does it take place? In Christ. How does it take place? By the blood. Three verses later, the apostle said, "And that he might reconcile both unto God in one body by the cross…" (v. 16). What is taking place? Being reconciled (same as redeemed and made near). Where does it take place? In one body

(same as being in Christ). How does it take place? By the cross (where blood was shed).

Now the question is how does one get into Christ? We are baptized into Christ (Gal. 3:27). How does one get into the one body? He is baptized into one body (1 Cor. 12:13).

The objections

1. **"One is saved by faith, thus it is not by baptism."** To refute the idea that baptism is essential, denominationalist often appeal to passages that say we are saved by faith and conclude that means baptism cannot be a condition for salvation. If faith eliminates baptism, it would also eliminate repentance. The passages that mention faith cannot mean salvation is by faith alone (Jas. 2:24). Examples can be found of those who believed, but were not saved (Jas. 2:19; John 8:31, 44).

2. **"One is saved by the blood of Christ, thus it is not by baptism."** Just like the previous objection, passages are cited that teach one is saved by the blood of Christ, so they conclude that baptism cannot be essential. If the passages that say salvation is by the blood of Christ mean that baptism is not essential, they also mean faith is not essential. The blood is *what* saves us; baptism is merely the *when*. We are washed in the blood (Rev. 1:5). Yet, baptism washes away sin (Acts 22:16). Remission of sins is by the blood of Christ (Matt. 26:28), but we are baptized for the remission of sins (Acts 2:38).

3. **"The thief on the cross was saved without baptism."** It is argued that since Jesus told one of the thieves on the cross, "…today you will be with Me in Paradise" (Luke 23:43), they conclude that we too can be saved without being baptized. It is not said that the thief repented. Does that mean that we don't have to repent (Acts 17:30-31)? It is not said that the thief believed that Jesus was raised from the dead. Does that mean we don't have to believe in the resurrected Christ? The thief lived and died under the Old Testament, before Jesus' commands (Mark 16:16) were in force (Heb. 9:16-17).

4. **"Cornelius (Acts 10) was saved without baptism because he received the Holy Spirit before he was baptized."** If the reception of the Holy Spirit proves salvation before baptism, it proves salvation before faith. The Spirit fell as Peter began to speak (Acts 11:15). That means that Cornelius and his household received the Spirit before they heard the message that produces faith (Rom. 10:17). This occurred at the beginning, not the end of the sermon. What this proved was not that they were saved without baptism, but that the Gentiles were gospel subjects (Acts 11:18).

The blood is *what* saves us; baptism is merely the *when*.

5. **"Mark 16:16 does not say 'and is not baptized' when describing the one that would be damned."** Not only would that not be necessary, it would be absurd. To be saved one must believe and be baptized. However, if one does not believe, he will not be baptized. That alone will cause him to be lost. Let's go back to our eating and digesting illustration: "He that eats and digests shall be healthy, but he that does not eat shall be unhealthy." Two things are essential to be healthy (eating and digesting). However, if one does not eat, he will not digest. There is no need (and it would be absurd) to say, "but he that does not eat and does not digest shall be unhealthy."

6. **"Mark 16:9-20 is not reliable since it is missing from some of the oldest manuscripts."** It is true that these verses are missing from the Codex Vaticanus and the Codex Sinaiticus (two of over 5,000 extant manuscripts). Interesting is the fact that Mark 16:9-20 is not all that is missing from those manuscripts. 1 Timothy through Philemon and Hebrews 9:14 through Revelation are missing from the Vaticanus. Matthew 1-24, parts of John and 2 Corinthians are missing from the Sinaiticus.

While missing from these two, Mark 16:9-20 is found in hundreds of manuscripts. In fact, the majority of the manuscripts contain it. The patristic writers ("church fathers") that contain these verses would include Irenaeus (2nd century), Eusebius (d. 339/340), and Jerome (d. 420). The 47 translators of the KJV, 101 of the ASV and 119 of the NKJV included it in the text.

The authenticity of these verses was never questioned, only its genuineness. That is, did Mark or some other writer pen it?

Every point found in verses 9-20 can be corroborated by other texts. There is not a single point in these verses that is not true.

Questions

1. What are some points that are often discussed (when we talk to our friends about baptism) that are not really the issue? _____

_____

_____

2. What is the real issue about the essentiality of baptism? _____

_____

_____

3. Why is it so important to discuss whether baptism is essential? _____

_____

_____

4. Can you think of some other illustrations or parallels to help understand Mark 16:16 besides those given in this lesson? _____

_____

_____

_____

5. For class discussion: Discuss the value of being simplistic in discussing this subject and perhaps sticking with one or two basic arguments or passages. _____
    _____
    _____
    _____

6. How can you prove that "for the remission of sins" (Acts 2:38) means "in order to obtain the remission of sins" and does not mean "because your sins have been forgiven?" _____
    _____
    _____

7. What is the comparison about Noah's day in 1 Peter 3:20-21? _____
    _____
    _____

8. How would you answer the objection that we are saved by faith, not by baptism? _____
    _____
    _____

9. How would you answer the objection that the thief on the cross was saved without being baptized? _____
    _____
    _____

10. How would you answer the objection that Cornelius was saved before he was baptized because he received the Holy Spirit before he was baptized? _____
    _____
    _____

11. How would you respond to the contention that Mark 16:9-20 is not supposed to be in the Bible? _____
    _____
    _____
    _____
    _____

WHY WE BELIEVE
One Is Not Saved by Faith Alone

Several religious groups believe and teach that one is saved by faith alone without any other conditions. Some would consistently believe salvation by faith only. Others say they believe in the doctrine of faith only, but still believe repentance is essential. One of the ways they try to harmonize that is to argue that repentance and faith are joined together and happen at the same time.

Pendleton's Baptist Church Manual says that the pardon of sins and the promise of eternal life comes, "solely through faith in the redeemer's blood" (p. 48). The Methodist discipline says, "Wherefore, that we are justified by faith, only, is a most wholesome doctrine and very full of comfort" (*The Book of Discipline of the United Methodist Church*, 1972 Edition, p. 55).

Those who believe this doctrine contend that passages that say one is saved by faith (i.e. Rom. 5:1) mean salvation by faith alone. They argue that if one is not saved by faith alone, then salvation is by works (cf. Eph. 2:8-9).

Let's consider several reasons why one is not saved by faith alone.

The Bible says it is not by faith only.

James wrote, "You see then that a man is justified by works, and not by faith only" (Jas. 2:24). The only time "faith only" is used in the Bible, it says we are *not* saved by faith only.

The same writer said, "Thus also faith by itself, if it does not have works, is dead" (Jas. 2:17). Then again he wrote, "For as the body without the spirit is dead, so faith without works is dead also (v. 26). Faith without works is a dead faith. Thus, if one is saved by faith only, one is saved by a dead faith!

Some believers are still lost.

There are many examples of people who believed but were not saved. The devils believe and tremble (Jas. 2:19). Jesus confronted some Jews who "believed on him" (John 8:31) but who were still children of the devil (v. 44). There were those who

> The only time **"faith only"** is used in the Bible, it says we are **not** saved by faith only.

believed but would not confess Christ, lest they be put out of the synagogue (John 12:42). If one is saved by faith alone, all of these would be saved.

The Bible requires other conditions.

1. **Repentance is required.** Repentance is essential to the remission of sins (Acts 2:38). It is required to have life (Acts 11:18). God commands all men to repent (Acts 17:30-31). If repentance is required, then salvation is not by faith only.

2. **Baptism is required.** Jesus said one must be baptized to be saved (Mark 16:16). Peter said it is essential to the remission of sins (Acts 2:38).

If God requires anything more than faith, salvation is not by faith only.

This doctrine has serious consequences.

If one is saved by faith only:

1. **Repentance would not be essential.** Yet many think that it is required.

2. **"Praying through" for salvation would not be essential.** Yet many think it is required. Often, those who talk about salvation by faith only encourage those who want to be saved to accept Jesus as their savior and pray the "sinners prayer." The Bible says nothing about the sinner's prayer or praying through for God to save you. Our point here is that those who claim salvation is by faith alone cannot truly accept the need for the sinner's prayer.

3. **Obedience is not essential.** One doesn't have to obey to be saved if it is all by faith alone. Yet Jesus said, "Not everyone who says to Me, 'Lord, Lord,' shall enter the kingdom of heaven, but he who does the will of My Father in heaven" (Matt. 7:21). Eternal salvation is promised to those who obey Christ (Heb. 5:8-9). Our souls are purified in obeying the truth (1 Pet. 1:22).

We are saved by works.

1. **We are saved by works.** (Acts 2:40; 10:35; Phil. 2:12; Jas. 2:24)

2. **We are not saved by works.** (Rom. 3:28; Eph. 2:9; Gal. 2:16)

3. **There are different kinds of works.** The Bible says we are saved by works and that we are not saved by works. To understand those passages, we must notice the various kinds of works mentioned in the Bible:

The Bible says nothing about the **sinner's prayer** or **praying through** for God to save you.

- **Works of the law of Moses** (Rom. 3:28; Gal. 2:16)

- **Works of faith** (1 Thess. 1:3)

- **Good works** (Eph. 2:10; Tit. 2:14)

- **Works of God** (John 6:28-29)

- **Works of God's righteousness** (Acts 10:35)

4. **We are *not* saved by...** works of the law (Rom. 3:28; Gal. 2:16), works of man's righteousness (Tit. 3:5; Eph. 2:9), or dead works (Heb. 6:1; 9:14).

5. **We *are* saved by...** works of God (John 6:28-29), works of God's righteousness (Acts 10:35), good works (Eph. 2:10; Tit. 2:14), and works of faith (1 Thess. 1:3).

Faith includes other acts of obedience.

1. **There is a common figure of speech (called *synecdoche*) wherein a part stands for the whole.** In other words, part of something is mentioned, though it is a reference to the whole of something. We use this form of speech all the time. We refer to our cars as "wheels." We may mention one person meaning the whole family. The same is true when The Bible mentions one condition for salvation.

   Jesus said those that "hear" shall live (John 5:25). Does that mean they don't have to believe—all they have to do is hear? Or, does "hear" stand for hearing and responding? The Gentiles were granted "repentance" unto life (Acts 11:18). That passage doesn't mention faith. Does that mean all that is required is repentance? No, repentance stands for obedience. The same is true of passages that say one is justified by faith (Rom. 5:1) or believe to be born of God (1 John 5:1).

2. **"Faith" or "believe" stands for obedience.** God told Moses to speak to the rock so it would bring forth water (Num. 20:8). However, Moses struck the rock. "Then Moses lifted his hand and struck the rock twice with his rod; and water came out abundantly, and the congregation and their animals drank" (v. 11). He did not obey! In the next verse God rebuked him saying, "Because you *did not believe Me*, to hallow Me in the eyes of the children of Israel, therefore you shall not bring this assembly into the land which I have given them" (v. 12; emphasis mine, DVR). Moses' disobedience was described as not believing. Thus, *believe* is used to stand for obedience.

   Paul described the Jews that were lost saying, "But they have not all *obeyed* the gospel. For Isaiah says, 'Lord, who has *believed* our report?'" (Rom. 10:16; emphasis mine, DVR).

A **synecdoche** is a figure of speech in which a term for a **part** of something is used to refer to the **whole** of something.

His point is that they had not obeyed. To prove that, he quotes Isaiah who talked about believing. Thus, here, "believe" stands for obedience.

3. **Salvation by faith includes repentance and baptism.** Cornelius was told to "believe" and he would receive the remission of sins (Acts 10:43). But, when Peter told the story in the next chapter the brethren concluded that the Gentiles have been granted "repentance unto life" (Acts 11:18). "Believe" in Acts 10:43 includes the "repentance" of Acts 11:18. *Believe* does not mean *believe alone* any more than *repentance* means *repentance alone.*

Paul told the Galatians, "You are the children of God by faith." The reason he could say that is "for" they had been baptized (Gal. 3:26-27).

Questions

1. How do some false teachers try to harmonize their doctrine of faith only with the requirement to repent?_____
    _____
    _____

2. What assumption is made (by those who believe in faith only) with every passage that talks about salvation by faith?_____
    _____
    _____

3. How many passages mention "faith only" and what do we learn from them? _____
    _____
    _____

4. What is the point made in this lesson about a dead faith? _____
    _____
    _____
    _____

5. Give some Bible examples of people who believed and yet were lost. _____
    _____
    _____
    _____

6. How do passages on repentance answer the question of salvation by faith only? _____
    _____
    _____

7. What are the serious consequences to the doctrine of salvation by faith alone? _____
    _____
    _____

8. Can you think of other consequences than the ones mentioned in this lesson?_____
    _____
    _____

9. How can we harmonize passages that say we are saved by works and those that say we are
    not saved by works? _____
    _____
    _____

10. What kind of works are under consideration in Romans 3:28? _____
    _____
    _____

11. What kind of works are under consideration in Ephesians 2:9? _____
    _____
    _____

12. What is synecdoche? _____
    _____
    _____

13. Give some examples where one condition of salvation is mentioned, but others are
    included. _____
    _____
    _____

14. Be prepared to develop (in class) the point made in this lesson from Romans 10:16. _____
    _____
    _____
    _____
    _____

WHY WE BELIEVE
Baptism Must Be Immersion

A very common practice in the religious world is to sprinkle or pour for baptism. This may be administered to adults, but it is especially administered to infants. In all of this, we hear discussion of "modes of baptism." The idea is that sprinkling, pouring and immersion are all different modes of baptism.

We must establish a distinction between "mode" and "action." Sprinkling, pouring and immersion are each a different action, not different modes or methods. If we want to talk about different modes of baptism we might think about the candidate standing, sitting or kneeling. One could be taken backwards, forward or sideways. All of these are different modes of the *same* action: immersion.

Let's consider several reasons why we believe baptism must be immersion.

Baptism is a burial.

1. **Baptism is called a burial.** Paul wrote, "Or do you not know that as many of us as were baptized into Christ Jesus were baptized into His death? Therefore we were *buried with Him through baptism* into death, that just as Christ was raised from the dead by the glory of the Father, even so we also should walk in newness of life" (Rom. 6:3-4; emphasis mine, DVR). Not only is baptism called a burial—notice the parallel that is drawn. Just as Jesus died, was buried and then raised, we die to sin, are buried in baptism, and then raised to a new life.

   The same writer said, "*buried with Him in baptism*, in which you also were raised with Him through faith in the working of God, who raised Him from the dead" (Col. 2:12; emphasis mine, DVR).

2. **Burial defined.** Bury means "to conceal by or as if by covering with earth…to place (a dead body in a grave, a tomb, or the sea…to cover from view…" (*American Heritage Dictionary*). Thus, if one is baptized (buried) in water, he is overwhelmed with water or completely covered with water.

> Just as Jesus died, was buried and then raised, we **die** to sin, are **buried** in baptism, and then **raised** to a new life.

baptisma: consisting of the processes of **immersion, submersion** and **emergence**

baptizo: 'to **dip**,' was used among the Greeks to signify the **dyeing of a garment**...

The word baptism means immersion.

The word baptism is not a translation, but a transliteration. That means, "to represent or spell in the characters of another alphabet" (Merriam-Webster.com). The noun form of the word is *baptisma*. The verb form is *baptizo*.

1. ***Baptisma* defined by W. E. Vine:** "1. *baptisma* NT:908, 'baptism,' consisting of the processes of immersion, submersion and emergence (from *bapto*, "to dip"), is used (a) of John's "baptism," (b) of Christian "baptism," see B. below; (c) of the overwhelming afflictions and judgments to which the Lord voluntarily submitted on the cross, e. g., Luke 12:50; (d) of the sufferings His followers would experience, not of a vicarious character, but in fellowship with the sufferings of their Master. Some mss. have the word in Matt 20:22-23; it is used in Mark 10:38-39, with this meaning."

2. ***Baptizo* defined by W. E. Vine:** "*baptizo* NT:907, 'to baptize,' primarily a frequentative form of *bapto*, 'to dip,' was used among the Greeks to signify the dyeing of a garment, or the drawing of water by dipping a vessel into another, etc. Plutarchus uses it of the drawing of wine by dipping the cup into the bowl (Alexis, 67) and Plato, metaphorically, of being overwhelmed with questions (Euthydemus, 277 D)."

3. ***Baptizo* defined by Joseph Henry Thayer:** "1. properly, to dip repeatedly, to immerge, submerge; 2. to cleanse by dipping or submerging, to wash, to make clean with water (Luke 11:38); 3. metaphorically, to overwhelm."

4. ***Baptizo* defined by *Strong's*:** "*baptizo* (bap-tid'-zo); from a derivative of NT:911; to immerse, submerge; to make overwhelmed (i.e. fully wet); used only (in the N. T.) of ceremonial ablution, especially (technically)."

5. ***Baptizo* defined by Walter Bauer (Gingrich and Danker):** "*baptizo* 'dip, immerse mid. dip oneself, wash (in non-Christian lit. also 'plunge, sink, drench, overwhelm'...)'"

Examples of baptism show the person going into the water.

1. **Jesus came up out of the water (Matt. 3:16).** "When He had been baptized, Jesus came up immediately from (out of, KJV) the water; and behold, the heavens were opened to Him, and He saw the Spirit of God descending like a dove and alighting upon Him" (Matt. 3:16). If he came out of the water, we must conclude that he went down into the water when he was baptized.

2. **Both Philip and the eunuch went down into the water (Acts 8:38).** "So he commanded the chariot to stand still. And both Philip and the eunuch went down into the water, and he baptized him" (Acts 8:38). Both going down into the water is not necessary for sprinkling or pouring, but would be for immersion.

3. **John baptized where there was much water (John 3:23).** "Now John also was baptizing in Aenon near Salim, because there was much water there. And they came and were baptized" (John 3:23). Much water is not essential for sprinkling or pouring, but is for immersion.

4. **Crowds came to the Jordan River to be baptized by John (Matt. 3:6; Mark 1:5).** Going out to the Jordan would not be necessary for sprinkling or pouring, but would be for immersion.

5. **The jailor left the jail house to be baptized (Acts 16:33).** Sprinkling or pouring could have been performed in the jail.

With immersion, the action is on the person, but with sprinkling and pouring, the action is on the water.

Sprinkling and pouring are not synonymous or parallel with immersion. In one the action is on the person and in the other the action is on the water.

1. **What is baptized?** It is men and women who are baptized (Acts 8:12). The action is on the person, not the water.

2. **What is sprinkled?** It is water that is sprinkled. Sprinkle means to scatter or disperse in small drops. Water is sprinkled on the person. The person is not sprinkled.

3. **What is poured?** It is water that is poured (to cause to flow in a stream). It is poured over the person, but the person is not poured. The water is.

4. **What is the direct object?** Sprinkling has as its direct object water. Pouring has as its direct object water. Immersion or baptism has as its direct object the person.

We must conclude that sprinkling or pouring are entirely different from immersion.

The candidates for baptism are penitent believers.

One reason for practicing sprinkling is that babies are "baptized." Let's consider whether babies should be baptized at all.

Much water is not essential for **sprinkling** or **pouring**, but is for **immersion**.

1. **Those being baptized are to be believers.** Jesus said, "He who believes and is baptized will be saved; but he who does not believe will be condemned" (Mark 16:16). When the eunuch wanted to know if he could be baptized he was told if he believed he could be (Acts 8:36-37). Before the Corinthians were baptized, they heard and believed (Acts 18:8).

2. **Those being baptized are to be penitent.** Peter said, "Repent, and let every one of you be baptized in the name of Jesus Christ for the remission of sins; and you shall receive the gift of the Holy Spirit" (Acts 2:38).

3. **Infants do not fit the Bible pattern for baptism.** They have not sinned (Ezek. 18). Baptism is for the remission of sins (Acts 2:38; 22:16). They cannot repent (Acts 2:38). They are not capable of repenting. Furthermore, there is no sin in their life of which they need to repent (Rom. 7:9). They are not capable of formulating faith in their heart (John 8:24). They are not able to look at the evidence and thus have faith (Rom. 10:17).

Questions

1. Is the issue here different modes of baptism? _____
   _____
   _____

2. Is it scriptural to practice different modes of baptism? _____
   _____
   _____

3. How does Romans 6:4 (and its context) help us answer the question of whether immersion is demanded? _____
   _____
   _____

4. What is a transliteration? How does it differ from translation? _____
   _____
   _____
   _____

5. What does *baptisma* mean? _____
   _____
   _____

6. What does *baptizo* mean? _____
   _____
   _____

7. What does the baptism of Jesus tell us about the question of sprinkling, pouring or immersion? _____
   _____
   _____

8. Why did John baptize near Jordan? What does that say about the question in this lesson?

    _____

    _____

9. How does the baptism of the eunuch answer the question of whether sprinkling or pouring
    is scriptural? _____

    _____

    _____

10. Explain the difference in the action on the person and action on the water and how that
    addresses the question of whether sprinkling or pouring is a form of baptism. _____

    _____

    _____

11. Who is a candidate for baptism? _____

    _____

    _____

12. How can we show that babies are not candidates for baptism? _____

    _____

    _____

WHY WE BELIEVE
There Is Only One Church

The common concept in the religious world is that it makes no difference what one believes or practices in religion, therefore one church is as good as another. Which church one is a part of is a matter of personal choice.

First, let's define what the church is. If we don't, confusion is created when one person thinks one thing and another has a different thing in mind.

The church is people. When Saul made havoc of the church, he did so by dragging off "men and women" (Acts 8:3). What he did to the men and women is what he did to the church.

The church is people who are saved. Those who were saved were added to the church (Acts 2:47). Those who are reconciled are in the one body (Eph. 2:16). Christ is the savior of the body (Eph. 5:23). Those whom he saves are in the body. Additionally, the terms of entrance are the same. That is, what one must do to be saved (i.e. Mark 16:16) is the same that one must do to enter into the church (i.e. 1 Cor. 12:13).

The term "church" comes from the Greek term *ekklesia*. It is a compound word. *Ek* means "out of" (from which we get the word exit). *Klesia* means "to call." Thus, it refers to those who are called out. Those who have been called by the gospel (2 Thess. 2:14), out of sin into salvation (Eph. 2), and out of darkness into light (1 Pet. 2:9) are those who are in the church.

ekklesia: the **church**; those who are **called out**

The church is called the house (family) of God (1 Tim. 3:15). Thus, to be a child of God one must be in the church.

Now that we know what the church is, let's consider why we believe there is just one church.

Jesus only promised to build one.

1. **Jesus said he would build his church.** The statement to Peter was, "I will build my church" (Matt. 16:18). Notice that the term church is singular in number. The promise was to build his "church" not "churches."

2. Every prophecy of the church or kingdom was for one. Isaiah spoke of the Lord's house, not houses (Isa. 2:1-4). Daniel foretold of a kingdom, not kingdoms (Dan. 2:44). The same prophet said the Son of Man would ascend to the Ancient of Days to be given "a kingdom," not kingdoms (Dan. 7:13-14). Micah prophesied about the Lord's house, not houses (Micah 4:1). Jesus said the kingdom (not kingdoms) would come with power (Mark 9:1). Our Lord taught his disciples to pray that the kingdom (not kingdoms) come (Matt. 6:10).

If there is more than one church, there are more than Jesus promised.

The Bible says there is just one.

1. Paul taught that there is one church. The apostle wrote, "there is one body" (Eph. 4:4). The same writer (in the same book) said the body is the church (1:22-23). Thus, there is one church!

2. The New Testament repeatedly states there is one body. We are members in the one body (Rom. 12:4-5). We are one bread and one body (1 Cor. 10:17). We are members of the one body (1 Cor. 12:12). We are baptized into one body (1 Cor. 12:13). Reconciliation takes place in one body (Eph. 2:16). We are called in one body (Col. 3:15).

If there is more than one church, there is more than the Bible says there is.

The Bible is silent about churches.

1. There is no passage that says anything about churches (plural) or denominations. Yes, there were a plurality of local congregations (Rev. 2-3), but that is not what we are discussing. We are talking about one church in contrast to denominationalism.

2. If the Bible is silent, then it is not the will of God. We must speak as the oracles of God (1 Pet. 4:11). The Hebrew writer said, "For it is evident that our Lord arose from Judah, of which tribe Moses spoke nothing concerning priesthood" (Heb. 7:14). God said nothing about those of the tribe of Judah being priests. Since he was silent, they could not be priests (cf. Heb. 8:4). The silence of God is not permissive, but prohibitive.

Like Timothy, we are charged to preach the word (2 Tim. 4:2). If it is not in the word of God, we cannot preach it. The idea of a plurality of churches or denominationalism is not in the word. Thus, it cannot be taught or practiced.

If churches (plural) are in the Bible, where is the passage?

The idea of a **plurality** of churches is not in the **word**. Thus, it cannot be **taught** or **practiced**.

It makes a difference what one believes.

In our first lesson we focused on the question of whether it makes a difference what one believes. Let's consider two points we made there and see how it fits with the question at hand.

1. **The Bible, the word of God, is the objective standard we have in religion.** All of the following are descriptions of that standard. We must abide by what is written of God (2 Cor. 4:13), the oracles of God (1 Pet. 4:11), the commandments of the Lord (1 Cor. 14:37), the word of God (1 Thess. 2:13), the inspired Scriptures (2 Tim. 3:16-17), and the words chosen by the Holy Spirit (1 Cor. 2:9-13).

    If there is an objective (fixed) standard, then it makes a difference what one believes. The principle also works in reverse. If it makes a difference what one believes, then there must be an objective standard we have to follow.

2. **Those who believe a lie will perish (2 Thess. 2:10-12).** Note the contrast in this passage between those who believe a lie and those who believe the truth. Those who believe the truth (v. 12) and love the truth (v. 10) will be saved (v. 10). However, those who are deceived (v. 10), deluded (v. 11) and believe a lie (v. 11) will perish (v. 10) and be condemned (v. 12). Thus, it makes a difference what one believes.

    If it makes a difference what one believes, then one church is not as good as another. Since it makes a difference, a church must follow the pattern of God (Heb. 8:5) and abide within the doctrine of Christ (2 John 9).

Division is wrong.

1. **Three reasons division is wrong:** First, Jesus prayed for unity (John 17:20-21). Second, Paul condemned division (1 Cor. 1:10). Third, division is contrary to the doctrine (Rom. 16:17-18).

2. **Denominationalism is division.** The word "denomination" means "the act of naming...the name of a class or group; classification" (*American Heritage Dictionary*). Thus, it refers to divisions or classifications. It is a term that previously was used in banking. Years ago, when you cashed a check, the teller would ask you, "What denomination?" She was not asking which church, but what division of money ($1, $5, $10, $20, $50 or $100).

3. **Three things are implied by the use of the term "denomination."** When used in banking, it suggests: (a) there is division. If money were not divided into $1, $5, $10, etc. the term "denomination" would not be used. Suppose that the only form of currency we had was one dollar bills. The teller

> Since it **makes a difference** what one believes, a church must **follow the pattern** of God and abide within the **doctrine of Christ**.

The word **denomination** implies:

- There is **division**.

- One group is as **good** as another.

- There are no **wrong** choices.

would never ask, "What denomination?" It also suggests: (b) that one (group) is as good as another. That doesn't mean that $1 is as good as $100. But, one classification is as good as another. In other words, the denomination of $1 (100 one dollar bills) is as good as the denomination of $100 (1 one hundred dollar bill). Furthermore: (c) there are no wrong choices. That is, if you tell the bank teller that you prefer to have your money in $20 bills, that is your choice; no one will condemn you. These same three principles apply to churches if denominationalism is true.

4. **The concept of denominationalism.** The idea of denominationalism is that God's people are divided into various sects or groups. Thus, some of God's people are Baptist, some are Methodist, some are Presbyterian, some are Nazarenes, some are Catholic, some are Adventist, etc. The same three points made above fit here. If this picture is true, then: (a) God's people are divided, (b) one is as good as another, and (c) there are no wrong choices.

5. **What is wrong with denominationalism?** (a) It is not found in the Bible (1 Pet. 4:11). (b) It is contrary to Jesus' and Paul's plea for unity (John 17:20-21; 1 Cor. 1:10). (c) It makes a difference what one believes (2 Thess. 2:10-12). (d) It is contrary to the idea of there being one body (Eph. 4:4).

There is a difference.

We need to clarify the difference in three terms and concepts.

1. **Denominational:** The idea of denominationalism (as noted above) is that God's people are divided into various sects. To be in a denomination, one must subscribe to that church's creed.

2. **Non-Denominational:** The idea here is that the church is not a part of any denomination or one of many denominations. This says that the church is singular. The Lord's church is non-denominational.

3. **Inter-Denominational:** The idea here is that the group accepts any and all. All believe different things, but still worship and work together. Many churches will advertise and claim to be "non-denominational." What they really mean is that they are inter-denominational. They will accept about anyone and anything.

What does all this mean?

If there is just one church, then you must be a part of that one church to be saved. Furthermore, it means that those in denominationalism must leave and renounce denominationalism.

Questions

1. Why is it important to clarify what the church is before answering the question of whether there is just one church? _____
    _____
    _____

2. How would you show that the church is people who are saved? _____
    _____
    _____

3. How does Jesus' promise to build his church answer the question of whether there are one or more churches? _____
    _____
    _____

4. How do the prophecies of the kingdom show us there is just one church? _____
    _____
    _____

5. How do you show that the one body is the one church? _____
    _____
    _____

6. What does the silence of God have to do with the question of one church? _____
    _____
    _____

7. How do you show that the silence of God is prohibitive? _____
    _____
    _____

8. Give three reasons division is wrong. _____
    _____
    _____

9. What three things are implied by the use of the term denomination? _____
    _____
    _____
    _____

10. What is the difference in denominational, non-denominational and inter-denominational?
    _____
    _____
    _____

WHY WE BELIEVE
Hell Is Real and Eternal

We begin with a summary of the Bible teaching on hell. It is a lake of fire (Rev. 20:10, 14, 15; 21:8). It is a furnace of fire (Matt. 13:42, 50). It is a flaming fire (2 Thess. 1:7-9). It is a baptism of fire (Matt. 3:11-12). It is an unquenchable fire (Mark 9:43, 48). It is described as brimstone (Rev. 21:8). There will be weeping, wailing and gnashing of teeth in hell (Matt. 8:12; 13:50). Hell was prepared for the devil and his angels (Matt. 25:41). It is outer darkness (Matt. 8:12; 25:30). There the wicked will be tormented forever and ever (Rev. 14:10-11).

Two questions we must address: (1) Is it real? (2) Is it eternal? The first we must answer because so many think hell is not a real place. Some think it is a myth. The second must be answered for there are those who claim hell is not eternal torment. Rather, the doctrine of annihilation says that one ceases to exist at death, thus there is no eternal punishment in hell. Others say that one who is wicked is punished for a while, and then ceases to exist.

Why we believe hell is real

1. **Jesus said it is real.** Jesus warned of the real possibility of being cast into hell. "If your hand causes you to sin, cut it off. It is better for you to enter into life maimed, rather than having two hands, to go to hell, into the fire that shall never be quenched—where 'Their worm does not die, And the fire is not quenched.'" (Mark 9:43-44).

   Hell is not a fictitious story used to scare people into submission. It is not a condition or state of mind. It is a place that is real.

   In the story of the rich man and Lazarus (Luke 16), the rich man died and went to Hades, the realm of departed spirits (v. 23). The torment he received (v. 23), is a foretaste of the greater to come in hell (*Gehenna*). This was a real place (vv. 23, 28).

   In the judgment scene in Matthew 25 Jesus said, "Then He will also say to those on the left hand, 'Depart from Me, you cursed, into the everlasting fire prepared for the devil and his angels'" (Matt. 25:41). The destiny of the wicked is the

Hell is not a **fictitious story** used to scare people into submission. It is not a **condition** or **state of mind**. It is a place that is **real**.

same as the devil and his angels. Angels that sinned suffer now and await future judgment (2 Pet. 2:4; Jude 6). That is real. The devil will be tormented day and night forever and ever (Rev. 20:10). That is real.

2. **It is placed on an equality with heaven.** Back to the judgment scene in Matthew 25: Jesus said, "And these will go away into everlasting punishment, but the righteous into eternal life" (v. 46). Heaven and hell both are referenced here. If one of these is real, then so is the other. If one is a myth, so is the other. If one is fictitious, then so is the other.

3. **It is something to be feared.** Jesus said, "And do not fear those who kill the body but cannot kill the soul. But rather fear Him who is able to destroy both soul and body in hell" (Matt. 10:28). Hell is to be feared more than someone taking your life. Thus, it must be real. Furthermore, it is something beyond the grave.

Why we believe hell is eternal

The question is, does the punishment of hell last forever and ever, or does the soul cease to exist?

1. **The same word describes heaven as eternal.** Notice again the statement of Jesus, "And these will go away into everlasting punishment, but the righteous into eternal life" (Matt. 25:46). The word everlasting (*aionios*) that describes punishment (hell) is the same word as eternal (*aionios*) that describes life (heaven). Hell is as eternal (lasts as long) as heaven. What we do with one, we must do with the other.

2. **The fire of hell is eternal, or everlasting.** Jesus warned, "If your hand or foot causes you to sin, cut it off and cast it from you. It is better for you to enter into life lame or maimed, rather than having two hands or two feet, to be cast into the everlasting fire" (Matt. 18:8). Sodom and Gomorrah were burned with fire, yet their punishment does not stop there. They will also suffer eternal fire (Jude 7). The soul doesn't go out of existence forever, but the fire (punishment) lasts forever (eternal, everlasting).

3. **Torment is forever.** The annihilationist teaches that the thing that is forever is the soul going out of existence. To the contrary, the text says, "the smoke of their torment ascends forever and ever" (Rev. 14:10-11). That same expression "forever and ever" is found in Revelation 4:9. There we learn that God lives "forever and ever." That means an endless future. The same is true when describing the torment (Rev. 14:11). It is an endless future.

The word **everlasting** (*aionios*) that describes punishment (hell) is the same word as **eternal** (*aionios*) that describes life (heaven). **Hell** is as eternal (lasts as long) as **heaven**.

4. **Fire is not quenched.** Jesus said, "If your hand causes you to sin, cut it off. It is better for you to enter into life maimed, rather than having two hands, to go to hell, into the fire that shall never be quenched—where 'Their worm does not die, And the fire is not quenched.'" (Mark 9:43-44; see also v. 46, 48; Isa. 66:24).

   What normally happens is that the worm eats the flesh of the animal. When the flesh is consumed, the worm dies. Normally when trash or rubbish is burned, it is consumed and the fire goes out. But in this text the worm does not die and fire is not quenched. That means it does not end. Hell does not end.

5. **The blackness of darkness is forever.** Jude wrote, "These are spots in your love feasts, while they feast with you without fear, serving only themselves. They are clouds without water, carried about by the winds; late autumn trees without fruit, twice dead, pulled up by the roots; raging waves of the sea, foaming up their own shame; wandering stars for whom is reserved the blackness of darkness forever." (Jude 12-13). Peter described some headed to their doom saying, "These are wells without water, clouds carried by a tempest, for whom is reserved the blackness of darkness forever" (2 Pet. 2:17). These passages teach that the blackness of darkness last forever.

   In outer darkness there is weeping and gnashing of teeth (Matt. 8:12; 22:13; 25:30). This is not annihilation. This is suffering that last forever and ever.

For these reasons we believe that hell is real and eternal.

Questions

1. Why is there a need to emphasize that hell is real? _____
   _____
   _____

2. Why is there a need to emphasize that hell is eternal? _____
   _____
   _____

3. Give three reasons why we believe hell is real. _____
   _____
   _____
   _____

4. How does the Hadean realm (Luke 16) help us to see that hell (*Gehenna*) is real? _____
   _____
   _____
   _____

5. What punishment awaits the devil? _____
   _____
   _____

6. What punishment awaits the devil's angels? _____
    _____
    _____

7. How are hell and heaven put on an equality? _____
    _____
    _____

8. What does the fact that the word "eternal" and "everlasting" (Matt. 25:46) comes from the same word tell us?_____
    _____
    _____

9. How can we show that it is suffering that last forever and not the soul ceasing to exist that is forever?_____
    _____
    _____

10. What does "where the worm does not die and the fire is not quenched" mean? _____
    _____
    _____

11. What connection is to be made between Jude 12-13 and Matthew 8:12? _____
    _____
    _____
    _____

WHY WE HAVE
The Lord's Supper Every Sunday

Jesus instituted the Lord's Supper as a memorial of his death. Paul's record of that stated, "For I received from the Lord that which I also delivered to you: that the Lord Jesus on the same night in which He was betrayed took bread; and when He had given thanks, He broke it and said, 'Take, eat; this is My body which is broken for you; do this in remembrance of Me.' In the same manner He also took the cup after supper, saying, 'This cup is the new covenant in My blood. This do, as often as you drink it, in remembrance of Me'" (1 Cor. 11:23-25).

The next verse says, "For as often as you eat this bread and drink this cup, you proclaim the Lord's death till He comes" (v. 26; emphasis mine, DVR). "As often as" suggests regularity (something done on a regular basis). That raises a question of how often, then, do we partake?

Common practices on frequency

It is not uncommon to find churches that offer the Lord's Supper once a month, once a quarter or once a year. An Internet search for "communion service," "communion schedule," or "communion Sunday" will reveal calendars or schedules showing which Sundays through the year the Lord's Supper will be offered.

In contrast, God's people have the Lord's Supper every Sunday. Is that a matter of preference or Bible principle?

The text

Any conclusions that are drawn about when and how often to partake of the Lord's Supper will be taken from Acts 20:7. That text says, "And upon the first day of the week, when the disciples came together to break bread, Paul preached unto them, ready to depart on the morrow; and continued his speech until midnight."

1. **Notice that the disciples were breaking bread on the first day of the week.** This is the only passage that tells us what day the Lord's Supper was observed.

Any conclusions that are drawn about **when** and **how often** to partake of the **Lord's Supper** will be taken from **Acts 20:7**.

We have no **command** about the day of observance, but we do have an **approved example**.

2. **This is an approved example.** We have no command about the day of observance, but we do have an approved example. How do we know that God approved of what they were doing here? As Paul preached on this occasion, Eutychus fell out of the window and died (v. 9). Paul raised him from the dead (a miracle) showing God's approval (vv. 10-12).

3. **"Break bread" refers to eating the Lord's Supper.** Some have questioned whether we can be sure "break bread" is referring to the Lord's Supper or a common meal. That expression (or at least the concept of breaking bread) is used multiple times to refer to the Lord's supper (Matt. 26:26; Mark 14:22; Luke 22:19; Acts 2:42; 1 Cor. 10:16; 11:23-24). It is also used to refer to a common meal (Acts 2:46). But how is it used in Acts 20:7?

This text (Acts 20:7) is a worship assembly. A common meal was not to be eaten in the assembly (1 Cor. 11:22). Thus, this is a reference to the Lord's Supper.

The first day of the week is a significant day.

1. **Jesus was raised from the dead on the first day of the week (Matt. 28:1; Mark 16:9).**

2. **Jesus appeared to his disciples on the first day of the week (John 20:19, 26).** Not only did he make appearances to those who initially saw him, but when the disciples (all but Thomas) met together (the very day he was raised) Jesus appeared in their midst (v. 19). A week later, they met again (Thomas was present this time) and Jesus appeared again (v. 26).

3. **The first gospel sermon was preached on the first day of the week (Acts 2).** The day of Pentecost fell on the first day of the week (Lev. 23:15-16). The first gospel sermon preached under the great commission was presented on that day.

4. **The church was established on the first day of the week (Acts 2:47).** The day of Pentecost was the first time the church was spoken of as already being in existence. All references before that time speak of it as in the future (Matt. 16:18). All reference after speak of it as already being established (Eph. 1:22-23; 5:32).

5. **The first day of the week was a day of worship for the first century disciples.** On the day of Pentecost (the first day of the week), disciples were found engaging in acts of worship (Acts 2:42). Christians met at Troas on the first day of the week to break bread (Acts 20:7). They would be assembled for worship on the first day, so Paul instructed that a collection be taken when they were assembled (1 Cor. 16:1-2).

The first day of the week means every first day of the week.

1. **Some translations of 1 Corinthians 16:2 say "on the first day of every week" (ESV, NASV, NIV, RSV, and NASUE).** Vincent says, "*Kata* (NT:2596) has a distributive force, 'every' first day" (Vincent Word Studies). Whether or not the word "every" should appear in the text is not the point, for Paul's instructions imply that it was to be done every time the first day rolls around.

2. **Illustrations.** Suppose a club posts this notice, "The club meets on Monday." What would that mean? Which Monday? We all understand that means every Monday. If, when you were hired, your boss said, "You will be paid on Friday," what would that mean? One Friday a year? One Friday a month? We all know that means every time there is a Friday. Suppose the boss says, "Saturday is double time." What would that mean? Which Saturday? Again, we know that means every time there is a Saturday.

3. **Since a day of the week is mentioned, then a weekly observance is what is intended.** Had God intended a yearly or annual observance, a day of the year would have been given (such as the first day of the second month). Had God intended a monthly observance, a day of the month would have been given (such as the tenth day of the month). Had God intended a weekly observance, a day of the week would have been given (such as the first day of the week, Acts 20:7).

Consider the following chart by David Pratte.[1]

> Since a **day of the week** is mentioned, then a **weekly observance** is what is intended.

Memorial/Feast	Scripture	Time	Frequency
Passover	Ex. 12:6,14,24ff	14th day, 1st month	Annual
Trumpets	Lev. 23:24	1st day, 7th month	Annual
Atonement	Lev. 23:27	10th day, 7th month	Annual
Tabernacles	Lev. 23:39-44	15th day, 7th month	Annual
Sabbath	Ex. 20:8-11	7th day of the week	Weekly
Lord's Supper	Acts 20:7	1st day of the week	Weekly

[1] http://www.gospelway.com/church/lords_supper_day.php

Parallel to the Sabbath day

1. **The Sabbath observance:** One of the Ten Commandments was, "Remember the Sabbath day to keep it holy" (Exo. 20:8). Which Sabbath day was to be remembered? The text did not say "every" Sabbath. However, that was understood. Every Jew understood that command to apply to every time the Sabbath day occurred.

2. **The Lord's Supper on the first day of the week:** When the first day of the week is mentioned in connection with the Lord's Supper, which first day does that mean? The same principle applies here that we see with the Sabbath day. Disciples are to break bread every time the first day of the week occurs.

The Sabbath day and the first day of the week come around every week.

Contrary evidence is lacking.

The evidence that the Lord's Supper is to be observed every week is found in Acts 20:7. Any evidence that it is to be observed once a month, once a year or quarterly has not been found. In the absence of evidence, we must stick with the revelation of God (1 Pet. 4:11).

Questions

1. What passage implies regularity in partaking of the Lord's Supper? _____
   _____
   _____

2. What is the common practice in the religious world concerning frequency of observing the Lord's Supper? _____
   _____
   _____

3. For class discussion: What are some churches in your area doing on the frequency of the communion? _____
   _____
   _____
   _____

4. How do you prove that "break bread" (Acts 20:7) refers to the Lord's Supper? _____
   _____
   _____

5. Why is the first day of the week so significant? _____
   _____
   _____

6. How do we know that the day of Pentecost fell on the first day of the week?_____
   _____
   _____

7. List some things that happened in Acts 2 that would be significant on the first day of the week. _____

_____

_____

8. Give some illustrations (both those in this lesson and some you can think of) that show the first day means every first day. _____

_____

_____

9. If God had intended an annual observance what would have to be revealed for us to know that? _____

_____

_____

10. If God had intended a monthly observance what would have to be revealed for us to know that? _____

_____

_____

11. If God had intended a weekly observance what would have to be revealed for us to know that? _____

_____

_____

12. Develop the point concerning the parallel with the command to observe the Sabbath. ___

_____

_____

WHY WE DON'T BELIEVE
Christ Will Reign on Earth for a Thousand Years

The doctrine of Premillennialism teaches that, when Christ returns, there will be a resurrection of the righteous, and then there will be a seven year rapture (righteous taken to heaven) while there are seven years of tribulation on earth (during which the antichrist reigns). At the end of the seven years there will be a judgment of the saints, the battle of Armageddon, the kingdom will be established, the temple will be rebuilt and the Jews will return to Palestine. Christ will return to sit on his literal throne for a thousand years. At the end of the thousand years, the wicked will be raised, and then the judgment.

Basic elements of the doctrine

1. **The kingdom is yet to be established.**

2. **The kingdom will be a literal, material kingdom.**

3. **Christ will come back and reign on a literal throne in Jerusalem.**

4. **There will be a thousand year reign of Christ on earth.**

5. **The Jews will return to Palestine.**

Let's consider several reasons why we don't believe Christ will reign on earth for a thousand years.

It is not in the Bible.

Quite often those who believe error will ask us to disprove their doctrine (which can be done). However, the burden of proof rests upon the one who believes a doctrine to prove it by the scriptures.

1. **We must believe and teach only what is found in the Bible.** Paul made an appeal to believe and speak according as it is written (2 Cor. 4:13). Peter urged us to speak as the oracles of God (1 Pet. 4:11).

2. **We must always check what we are taught by the Bible.** Never accept what anyone teaches without checking it by the Bible. The Bereans were commended because they searched the Scriptures to see if what they were taught was so (Acts 17:11). John wrote, "Beloved, do not believe every spirit, but

> The **burden of proof** rests upon the one who believes a doctrine to **prove it** by the scriptures.

test the spirits, whether they are of God; because many false prophets have gone out into the world" (1 John 4:1). How that is done is revealed five verses later (v. 6). If the doctrine agrees with the apostles' teachings, it is truth; if not, it is error.

3. **The doctrine that teaches that Christ will return and reign on earth for a thousand years is just not found in the Bible.** Without biblical evidence, we cannot accept it as true.

The kingdom has been established.

Premillennialists teach that the kingdom is to be established in the future. If we can show that the kingdom has already been established, then the doctrine is false.

1. **Daniel prophesied that the kingdom would be established during the Roman Empire (Dan. 2:44).** Daniel interpreted a dream that the Babylonian king had. Daniel told the king what his dream was:

You, O king, were watching; and behold, a great image! This great image, whose splendor was excellent, stood before you; and its form was awesome. This image's head was of fine gold, its chest and arms of silver, its belly and thighs of bronze, its legs of iron, its feet partly of iron and partly of clay. You watched while a stone was cut out without hands, which struck the image on its feet of iron and clay, and broke them in pieces. Then the iron, the clay, the bronze, the silver, and the gold were crushed together, and became like chaff from the summer threshing floors; the wind carried them away so that no trace of them was found. And the stone that struck the image became a great mountain and filled the whole earth. This is the dream. Now we will tell the interpretation of it before the king (Dan. 2:31-36).

When he explained the dream, Daniel said to Nebuchadnezzar, "you are this head of gold" (v. 38). Then he added, "But after you shall arise another kingdom inferior to yours; then another, a third kingdom of bronze, which shall rule over all the earth. And the fourth kingdom shall be as strong as iron, inasmuch as iron breaks in pieces and shatters everything; and like iron that crushes, that kingdom will break in pieces and crush all the others" (vv. 39-40).

Four world empires were represented in the dream. They were: the Babylonian Empire (gold), the Medo-Persian Empire (silver), the Greek Empire (Bronze), and the Roman Empire (iron and clay).

The prophet then said, "And in the days of these kings the God of heaven will set up a kingdom which shall never be destroyed; and the kingdom shall not be left to other people; it shall break in pieces and consume all these kingdoms, and it shall stand forever" (v. 44). Thus, the

The four world empires of Daniel's interpretation:

- **Babylonian**

- **Medo-Persian**

- **Greek**

- **Roman**

kingdom would be established in the days of the Roman Empire. It has already been established.

2. **Some in the time of Christ would live to see the kingdom (Matt. 16:28; Mark 9:1).** If the kingdom came in the time of those then living, it has already been established.

3. **Some in Paul's day were in the kingdom (Col. 1:13).** These were translated out of darkness into the kingdom of Christ. If they were in the kingdom, it has been established.

The church and the kingdom are one and the same. They have the same head. Christ is the head of the church (Col. 1:18) and the king of the kingdom (Col.1:13). They have the same subjects and territory. People from all nations come into the church (Rom. 1:5) and into the kingdom (Acts 2:39). The terms of entrance are the same. One is baptized into the church (1 Cor. 12:13) and born of the water to enter the kingdom (John 3:3, 5). The gospel is the law of the church (Rom. 1:15) and the law of the kingdom (Matt. 4:23). The Lord's Supper is a memorial for the church (1 Cor. 11:23-26) and in the kingdom (Luke 22:29-30).

Jesus used the terms *church* and *kingdom* interchangeably. "And I also say to you that you are Peter, and on this rock I will build My *church*, and the gates of Hades shall not prevail against it. And I will give you the *keys of the kingdom* of heaven, and whatever you bind on earth will be bound in heaven, and whatever you loose on earth will be loosed in heaven" (Matt. 16:18-19; emphasis mine, DVR). If I said, "I will build my house, and I will give you the keys to my dwelling," you understand that "house" and "dwelling" are one and the same. Why would Jesus build one thing and give the keys (terms of entrance) to something else?

> Jesus used the terms **church** and **kingdom** interchangeably.

Christ is on David's throne in heaven.

1. **The throne on which Christ sits is in heaven.** Daniel foretold that the Son of Man received a kingdom when he ascended to the Ancient of Days (Dan. 7:13-14). Furthermore, Christ would be a king and a priest on his throne (Zech. 6:12-13). If he were on earth, he could not be a priest (Heb. 8:4). Thus, if he were on earth, he could not be a king! The Psalmist said David's throne is established forever in heaven (Psa. 89:35-37, KJV).

2. **Christ is on his throne now.** Remember, he is a king and priest on his throne (Zech. 6:12-13). Thus, he is a king and a priest at the same time. He is a priest now (Heb. 4:14-15; 8:1-4). Thus, he is a king now. Peter's sermon declared that he is now sitting at the right hand of God (Acts 2:30-36).

   If Christ is on his throne in heaven, then his kingdom is not in the future and here on earth.

The second coming **ends** Christ's reign rather than **begins** His reign.

The second coming ends Christ's reign.

No one knows the day or the hour Christ will return (Matt. 24:36; Mark 13:32). He will come as a thief in the night (1 Thess. 5:2; 2 Pet. 3:9-10). When he does come, that will bring an end to his reign.

1. **When Christ returns his reign on his throne will end as he delivers the kingdom to the Father.** Paul said, "But each one in his own order: Christ the firstfruits, afterward those who are Christ's at His coming. Then comes the end, when He delivers the kingdom to God the Father, when He puts an end to all rule and all authority and power" (1 Cor. 15:23-24). The second coming ends his reign rather than begins his reign.

2. **The earth and all things will be burned up at the second coming.** Peter said, "The Lord is not slack concerning His promise, as some count slackness, but is longsuffering toward us, not willing that any should perish but that all should come to repentance. But the day of the Lord will come as a thief in the night, in which the heavens will pass away with a great noise, and the elements will melt with fervent heat; both the earth and the works that are in it will be burned up" (2 Pet. 3:9-10).

There is no promise that the Jews will return to Palestine.

1. **The land of Palestine was promised to Abraham and his seed (Gen. 13:15; 15:18; 17:7-8).** The premillennialists teach that the promise is yet to be fulfilled.

2. **The promise has been fulfilled.** Joshua tells us that all the land was given as promised.

   So the LORD gave to Israel all the land of which He had sworn to give to their fathers, and they took possession of it and dwelt in it. The LORD gave them rest all around, according to all that He had sworn to their fathers. And not a man of all their enemies stood against them; the LORD delivered all their enemies into their hand. Not a word failed of any good thing which the LORD had spoken to the house of Israel. All came to pass (Josh. 21:43-45).

   Behold, this day I am going the way of all the earth. And you know in all your hearts and in all your souls that not one thing has failed of all the good things which the LORD your God spoke concerning you. All have come to pass for you; not one word of them has failed. Therefore it shall come to pass, that as all the good things have come upon you which the LORD your God promised you, so the LORD will bring upon you all harmful things, until He has destroyed you from this good land which the LORD your God has given you. When you have transgressed the covenant of the LORD your God, which He commanded you, and have gone and served other gods, and bowed down to them, then the anger of the LORD will burn against you, and you shall perish quickly from the good land which He has given you (Josh. 23:14-16).

The territory over which Solomon reigned shows that the land promise had been fulfilled (1 Kings 4:21; 2 Chron. 9:26).

There is no promise in the Bible that the Jews will return to Palestine or that the land is theirs.

Revelation 20 does not teach it.

Those who believe that Christ will return to earth and reign in his kingdom for a thousand years appeal to Revelation 20:4 which says, "And they lived and reigned with Christ for a thousand years."

1. **This is signified (symbolic) language.** The book begins on the note that it is written in figurative language (Rev. 1:1). Thus, everything in the book is not to be taken literally.

2. **There are a number of things in Revelation 20 that are not literal.** There is a bottomless pit (v. 1), a great chain (v. 1), a dragon (v. 2) and a serpent (v. 2). If these are not literal, why should the thousand years be literal?

3. **Things not found in Revelation 20:** There are several things that would be part of the premillennial concept that are not found in this context. They include: the second coming, a bodily resurrection, the reign of Christ on earth, the Jews returning to Palestine, Christ returning to set foot on earth, Jerusalem, and a literal throne of David.

This doctrine cannot be established from Revelation 20:4.

Consequences

Every doctrine has consequences which the believer must accept or else give up the doctrine. Those who accept premillennialism face the following consequences.

1. **Christ is not priest now (Zech. 6:12-13).** If he is not king now, he cannot be priest now.

2. **One cannot observe the Lord's Supper since it is for those in the kingdom (Luke 22:29-30).**

3. **One cannot be born again now (John 3:3, 5).** If the kingdom does not exist yet, then one cannot be born again.

4. **All are in darkness now (Col. 1:13).** Since one who is delivered from darkness is in the kingdom, and the kingdom is yet future, then all are in darkness now.

5. **None are being converted now (Matt. 18:3).** When one is converted, he enters the kingdom. But if there is no kingdom yet, then none are being converted yet.

> If the bottomless pit, the great chain, the dragon and the serpent are **not literal**, why should the **thousand years** be literal?

Questions

1. Explain the doctrine of Premillennialism. _____

    _____

    _____

2. What was Nebuchadnezzar's dream (Dan. 2)? _____

    _____

    _____

3. What was Daniel's interpretation of Nebuchadnezzar's dream? _____

    _____

    _____

4. How can we prove that the kingdom has been established? _____

    _____

    _____

5. Give evidence that the church and the kingdom are one and the same. _____

    _____

6. What do we learn from Zechariah 6:12-13 that refutes the concepts of premillennialism?

    _____

7. Give evidence that the throne of Christ is in heaven. _____

    _____

8. Give evidence that Christ is on his throne now._____

    _____

9. What happens at the second coming to the reign of Christ? _____

    _____

10. What passages teach that the land promise to Abraham has been fulfilled? _____

    _____

    _____

11. How would you respond to those who cite Revelation 20:4 as evidence that Christ will reign on earth for a thousand years? _____

    _____

    _____

12. Can you think of some serious consequences to this false doctrine that are not listed in this lesson? _____

    _____

    _____

WHY WE DON'T USE
Instrumental Music in Worship

One of the most common questions we are asked is why we don't have mechanical instruments of music in worship. It is not because we don't like it. If it were a matter of personal like or dislike, we might use it. It is not because we can't afford it. Certainly if we could afford a nice building, we could afford a piano or organ. Neither do we oppose it because we have never had it.

So, why do we oppose instrumental music in worship?

There is no Bible authority for it.

1. **We must have Bible authority for all we do in religion.**
   God, because he is God, has authority over man (Gen. 1:1). Thus, we must abide by his authority. All that we do in word or deed is to be in the name of Christ (Col. 3:17). To act in the name of another means to act by his authority or power (Acts 4:17). John tells us that we must abide within the doctrine of Christ (2 John 9). The Hebrew writer tells us that Moses was instructed to make the tabernacle "according to the pattern" (Heb. 8:5). The tabernacle was the type or shadow (model) of the greater to come. If the type or shadow has to be made according to the pattern, how much more so the real and the true! Also, Jesus is the head of the church (Col. 1:18). Thus, the church is to take all direction from its head, Jesus Christ.

2. **How to determine Bible authority.** When some false teachers went to Antioch teaching that circumcision is essential to salvation, it was determined that Paul and Barnabas should go to Jerusalem to the apostles and elders (Acts 15:1-6). The discussion that followed concluded that Gentiles could be saved without being circumcised (v. 24). The decision was made by the Holy Spirit (v. 28).

   The speeches that were made used three methods to determine what the Holy Spirit's decision was concerning **Gentiles and circumcision**.

   Peter's speech (vv. 7-11) used *necessary inference*. Peter told about his experience at the house of Cornelius

> If the **type** or **shadow** has to be made according to the **pattern**, how much more so the **real** and the **true**!

Three methods
of determining
Bible authority:

- **Necessary inference**

- **Approved examples**

- **Command or direct statement from God**

(Acts 10-11). Peter learned that he was to take the gospel to the house of Cornelius from the following four events: (a) the heavenly vision (10:9-16), (b) the Spirit's instruction to follow the men who were sent for him (10:19-20), (c) the story of the angel at Cornelius's household (v. 22), and the Holy Spirit falling upon the house of Cornelius as Peter began to speak (10:44-47; 11:15).

He was not commanded to go the Gentiles. Rather, Peter *inferred* from these events that the Gentiles are gospel subjects as well as Jews. Notice how he began his sermon at Cornelius' household. He said, "I *perceive* that God shows no partiality" (10:34; emphasis mine, DVR). That is a matter of necessary inference. He concluded his sermon by saying, "Can anyone forbid water, that these should not be baptized who have received the Holy Spirit just as we have" (v. 47). Again, he *inferred* from the reception of the Holy Spirit that the Gentiles can be saved just like the Jews.

Peter went to Jerusalem and retold the story (Acts 11). He told them "If therefore God gave them the same gift as He gave us when we believed on the Lord Jesus Christ, who was I that I could withstand God?" (v. 17). "To have withstood God would have been to refuse to accept the necessary implications of the Holy Spirit's coming to Cornelius' household."[1] The Jews who heard him recount these events *concluded* (inferred), "Then God has also granted to the Gentiles repentance to life" (v. 18).

Where in Acts 10 or 11 was Peter *commanded* to preach to the Gentiles? Rather, he learned that by *inference*.

When Peter came to the Jerusalem discussion (Acts 15) he told about the Holy Spirit falling upon the house of Cornelius (vv. 7-8). He *deduced* that God "made no distinction between us and them, purifying their hearts by faith" (v. 9).

Paul and Barnabas' speech (v. 12) used *approved examples*. They told about the examples of them preaching among the Gentiles with God's approval (miracles and wonders). This is a reference to their work in the first missionary journey (Acts 13-14). The miracles at Paphos (13:8-12), Iconium (14:3), and Lystra (14:8-10) demonstrated that their example of preaching to Gentiles was approved.

James's speech (vv. 13-21) used *command or direct statement from God*. James appealed to Amos 9:11-12 which specifically said that those who may seek the Lord included the Gentiles (v. 17).

[1] D. E. Koltenbah, *Truth Magazine*, XI: 11 pp. 15-18, August 1967

Each one of these arguments stands independent of the other.

These methods of determining what is authorized can be illustrated with the **Lord's Supper**.

> **Command:** We learn about the *observance of the Lord's supper* because of a command: "this do in remembrance of me" (1 Cor. 11:24).
>
> **Example:** We learn about the *time of observance* from an approved example (Acts 20:7). Examples are binding (1 Cor. 4:6; 11:1; Phil. 3:17; 4:9; Heb. 6:12). Much is said about how we know when an example is binding. "The difficulties of the problem (if indeed the problem be so difficult) cannot be cited to negate the possibility of the authority of apostolic examples… It is neither scriptural nor rational to deny the validity of the argument from approved apostolic example because of an alleged problem in hermeneutics. Because the wheat must be separated from the chaff, so to speak, we do not solve the harvesting problem by plowing under the entire crop."[2]
>
> If we reject examples as binding authority on the basis that we have to determine which examples are binding and which are not, "then by the same token it is rational to reject out of hand any and all commands as binding because of the analogous difficulty in determining which commands are permanently binding. But if the latter is not rational, then neither is the former!"[3]
>
> **Necessary inference:** We learn about the *frequency of observance* from necessary inference (Acts 20:7). Just as "remember the Sabbath day and keep it holy" (Exo. 20:8) meant every time the Sabbath occurred, we conclude that the first day of the week means every time the first day occurs.

There is no command, example or necessary inference that authorizes the use of **instrumental music**.

God's silence is prohibitive.

1. **There are two mindsets concerning the silence of God.** One thought is that the silence of God is *permissive*. That is, that we are at liberty to do what is not condemned. In other words, if God did not say *not* to, we can do it. The other concept is that the silence of God is *prohibitive*. That is, we are forbidden to act without authority. Thus, we are not at liberty to act just because God has not specifically forbidden some act. These two mindsets have been at the heart of every major division within the body of Christ.

We are not at **liberty** to act just because God has not **specifically forbidden** some act.

[2] Koltenbah, *ibid.*
[3] D. E. Koltenbah, *Truth Magazine*, XI: 10, pp. 18-24, July 1967

2. **The silence of God is prohibitive.** The Hebrew writer said, "For it is evident that our Lord arose from Judah, of which tribe Moses spoke nothing concerning priesthood" (Heb. 7:14).

Since God is silent about the use of instrumental music, we are not authorized to use it.

God specified singing.

1. **Every passage that mentions music says "sing" or some equivalent.** Let's look at the passages:

   Matthew 26:30 – "sung"

   Mark 14:26 – "sung"

   Acts 16:25 – "sang"

   Romans 15:9 – "sing"

   1 Corinthians 14:15 – "sing"

   Ephesians 5:19 – "singing"

   Colossians 3:16 – "singing"

   Hebrews 2:12 – "sing"

   Hebrews 13:15 – "fruit of lips"

   James 5:13 – "sing"

2. **When God gives specific commands, man is not at liberty to choose other specifics within the generic realm.** For example, when God gave instructions to Noah to build an ark, he said to make the ark of gopher wood (Gen. 6:14). Had God said to make the ark of wood, Noah could have used any type of wood. However, in that God specified "gopher wood," Noah was not at liberty to use any other wood.

   The same is true of Elisha's instructions to Naaman to wash in the river of Jordan (2 Kings 5:10-12). Had God told him to wash in a river, then any river would have sufficed. However, in that Jordan was specified, all other rivers were eliminated. Naaman understood that (vv. 11-12).

   The offering for the leper specified that a lamb was to be used (Lev. 14:12-13). Had God said offer an animal, then any animal would have done (lamb, goat, bull, or a heifer). In that God specified a lamb, then, only a lamb would be acceptable.

   If we can understand these instructions, surely we can see the same when it comes to music in worship. Had God commanded music, man would be at liberty to choose any

Had God commanded **music**, man would be at liberty to choose **any kind of music** he wished.

kind of music he wished. However, God specified singing (Eph. 5:19). Thus, no other kind of music can be used.

If I were to give you money and tell you to go buy me a cola, you would be at liberty to choose any kind of cola (Coke, Pepsi, RC, etc.). Yet, if I specify Pepsi Cola, all other colas have been eliminated.

Command	Generic	Specific
Build ark (Gen. 6:14)	Wood	Gopher
Wash seven times (2 Kings 5)	River	Jordan
Offer (Lev. 14:12-13)	Animal	Lamb
Praise (Eph. 5:19)	Music	Sing
"Buy me a canned drink"	Cola	Pepsi

Instrumental music is an addition.

1. **We must not add to or take from the word of God.** Moses wrote, "You shall not add to the word which I command you, nor take anything from it, that you may keep the commandments of the LORD your God which I command you" (Deut. 4:2). We should have the attitude of Balaam when he said, "Though Balak were to give me his house full of silver and gold, I could not go beyond the word of the LORD my God, to do less or more" (Num. 22:18). The Proverb writer recorded, "Every word of God is pure; He is a shield to those who put their trust in Him. Do not add to His words, Lest He rebuke you, and you be found a liar" (Prov. 30:5-6). Perhaps we are most familiar with these words at the end of Revelation, "For I testify to everyone who hears the words of the prophecy of this book: If anyone adds to these things, God will add to him the plagues that are written in this book; and if anyone takes away from the words of the book of this prophecy, God shall take away his part from the Book of Life, from the holy city, and from the things which are written in this book" (22:18-19).

2. **Aids are authorized; additions are not.** Aids are authorized within the command (or example or necessary inference). When an aid is used, we are doing nothing more than what God said. However, when **another element** is added, we now have an addition.

We should have the **attitude of Balaam** when he said, "...I could not **go beyond** the word of the LORD my God, to do **less** or **more.**"

Consider the command to eat the **Lord's Supper** (1 Cor. 11:24). As we obey the command, we might use a table or plates to aid in carrying out the command. However, if we put jelly, beef or cola on the Lord's Table, another element has been added and thus we have an addition.

Obeying the command to **baptize** (Matt. 28:19) might require that we use an aid (a river, a baptistry or a heater). When we do that, we are doing nothing more than what God said: baptize. Suppose we decide to sprinkle. Now another action has been introduced, and that is an addition.

Let's go back to the command to **build an ark** (Gen. 6:14). If Noah used tools or some animal (to drag materials to the building site) he would simply be doing what God said—building an ark. Yet, if he decided to use oak or cedar wood, that would be an addition (since an additional element would be added).

In the matter of the **contribution** (1 Cor. 16:1-2), a congregation might use baskets to collect and an account to handle the money. Again, they are doing nothing more than what God said. If they were to take up a collection on another day (Monday or Saturday), another element has been added. That would be an addition.

The same is true with the command to **sing** (Eph. 5:19). When we use song books, pitch pipes, tuners and electronic hymnals, we are doing nothing more than what God said: sing. If, however, we use mechanical instruments of music, we have added another kind of music, which is an addition to the word of God.

> When we use song books, pitch pipes, tuners and electronic hymnals, we are doing **nothing more** than what God said: **sing**.

Command	Aid	Addition
Eat bread (1 Cor. 11)	Table, plates	Jam, beef, cola
Baptize (Matt. 28:19)	Baptistry, heater	Sprinkling
Build an ark (Gen. 6:14)	Tool, animal	Oak, cedar
Sing (Eph. 5:19)	Books, tuner	Instrumental music
Contribute (1 Cor. 16)	Basket, account	Monday, Saturday

3. **Let's consider a parallel.** If we can justify instrumental music, we can justify putting jam or jelly on the Lord's Supper bread. When someone says they want instrumental

music because they like it, we must remind them that we should have jam on the unleavened bread because someone likes it.

When it is contended that the instrument is just an aid to help make the singing better, we could argue the same for putting jam on the bread in the Lord's Supper.

Someone is sure to argue that we can have instrumental music because God didn't say *not* to use it. Likewise, God didn't say *not* to put jam on the unleavened bread.

"Psallo" does not authorize it.

The Greek verb *psallo* is used five times in the New Testament. It is translated "sing" (Rom. 15:9), "sing" (1 Cor. 14:15, twice), "make melody" (Eph. 5:19), and "sing psalms" (Jas. 5:13). The noun form of the same word (*psalmos*) is translated "psalms" (Luke 20:32; 24:44; Acts 1:20; 13:33; 1 Cor. 14:26; Eph. 5:19; Col. 3:16).

Those who contend that mechanical instruments of music are Scriptural have argued that the word *psallo* justifies the instruments. Their argument says that the word means to pluck or twang. They point out that the lexicons say it is used of playing a stringed instrument. Thus, they contend that instrumental music *inheres* in the word *psallo*.

1. **The meaning of the word:** Literally, the word means: "a. to pluck off, pull out; b. to cause to vibrate by touching, to twang" (Thayer). W. E. Vine: "To twitch, twang." Strongs: "probably strengthened from *psao* (to rub or touch the surface; compare NT:5597); to twitch or twang." Liddell and Scott: "to touch sharply, to pluck, pull, twitch, to pluck."

   It is used of plucking hair, a bowstring or a carpenter's line (Liddell and Scott). It is also used of plucking the strings of an instrument (Liddell and Scott, Thayer). It is used of singing by touching the cords of the heart (Thayer). So, yes the term can be used to refer to plucking the strings of an instrument.

   The object of the verb does not inhere in the verb. The verb means to pluck, twitch, or twang. It does not tell us what is to be plucked. The *what* is to be determined by the context.

   If the instrument of music (stringed instruments) *inheres* in the word, why doesn't "hair" inhere in the word since the lexicons say it can be used of plucking hair? Why doesn't a "bowstring" inhere in the word? Why doesn't the "carpenter's line" inhere in the term?

   In the New Testament the word means to sing. Notice what Vine's says about how the term is used in the New

> The verb **psallo** means to pluck, twitch, or twang. It does not tell us **what** is to be plucked. The **object** of the verb is specified in Ephesians 5:19: "...making melody **in your heart**."

Testament: "primarily to twitch, twang; then, to play a stringed instrument with the fingers, and hence, in the Sept., to sing with a harp, sing psalms; denotes, in the NT, to sing a hymn, sing praise; in Eph 5:19, making melody (for the preceding word *ado*, see SING). Elsewhere it is rendered sing; Rom 15:9; 1 Cor 14:15; in James 5:13, RV, let him sing praise (KJV, let him sing psalms)."

Thayer says essentially the same thing: "in the New Testament to sing a hymn, to celebrate the praises of God in song, Jas. 5:13; in honor of God, Eph. 5:19; Rom. 15:9."

2. **Missing evidence:** There is no lexicon that tells us that mechanical instruments of music *inhere* in the term *psallo*. There is no legitimate translation that translates the term as playing on mechanical instruments.

3. **The instrument is the heart.** The object of the verb is specified in Ephesians 5:19: "...making melody *in your heart*" (emphasis mine, DVR).

4. **If the instrument inheres in *psallo*, then it *must* be used and not merely serve as an aid.** It would be required of all worshipers and not just one who plays for the whole congregation. If plucking the strings of an instrument *inheres* in the term, then we must use a harp or stringed instrument.

Questions

1. How would you answer the person who says we don't have to have Bible authority for what we do in religion?_____
   _____
   _____
   _____

2. When the decision was made in Acts 15 (concerning circumcision), who made the decision? _____
   _____

3. How did Peter establish his point about circumcision (Acts 15:7-11)? _____
   _____
   _____

4. How did Paul and Barnabas establish their point about circumcision (Acts 15:12)?_____
   _____
   _____

5. How did James establish his point about circumcision (Acts 15:12)? _____
   _____
   _____

6. What are the two mindsets (concerning the silence of God) that create division? _____
   _____
   _____

7. How would you answer the contention that when God is silent (didn't tell us not to do something) that we are at liberty to do what is not forbidden? _____
    _____
    _____

8. Be prepared to list in class all the passages that mention "sing" or some equivalent. _____
    _____
    _____

9. What is the difference in generic and specific authority? _____
    _____
    _____

10. Since God specified "singing", how does that tell us not to use instrumental music? _____
    _____
    _____

11. What is the difference between an aid and an addition? _____
    _____
    _____

12. What is the argument made from *psallo*? _____
    _____
    _____

13. Show that the instrument does not inhere in the word *psallo*. _____
    _____
    _____

WHY WE BELIEVE
Miracles Have Ceased

Several religious groups believe in miracles today. Pentecostals, Charismatics, Nazarenes and some Baptists, among others, believe in miracles today. Some rely on miracles for healing, and therefore would not seek medical help. Others will seek medical help, and then claim that any healing is a miracle. Some have faith healing services (i.e. Oral Roberts, in years past) wherein there is a campaign to heal the masses of the sick.

Those who believe that miracles are still present today believe that Holy Spirit baptism (as the apostles had) is for believers today.

Let's consider why we believe miracles have ceased.

The purpose is accomplished.

1. **The miracles performed in the New Testament were not merely for the betterment of man.** Not all with whom the apostles came in contact were healed. Would it not seem likely that the apostles would have had large healing campaigns or "dead raising sessions" if the miracles were merely to improve man's condition?

2. **Miracles were for the confirmation of the message or claim.** When Jesus sent his apostles out, the text says, "And they went out and preached everywhere, the Lord working with them and confirming the word through the accompanying signs" (Mark 16:20). The work of confirmation has been accomplished. The word was confirmed (Heb. 2:3-4). Thus, there is no need for further confirmation.

3. **The Holy Spirit came upon the apostles to reveal the word.** The Spirit would guide the apostles in to all truth (John 16:13). The Spirit would teach them all things (John 14:26). There is no need for further revelation since the word of God is complete (Jude 3; 2 Pet. 1:3).

4. **The Holy Spirit coming upon the Gentiles proved that the Gentiles are now gospel subjects (Acts 11:18).** There is no need for additional proof that the Gentiles can be saved as the Jews.

There is no need for **further revelation** since the word of God is **complete**.

Since the purpose has ceased, we must conclude that the miracles have ceased.

Holy Spirit baptism has ceased.

1. **There are two cases of Holy Spirit baptism in the New Testament.** The first case is the apostles. The promise of Holy Spirit baptism was given to the apostles (Acts 1:4-5). On the day of Pentecost, it was the apostles who received the Spirit and spoke in tongues (Acts 2:1-4). Notice that the "they" and "them" in these verses who were filled with the Spirit refer to the nearest antecedent, the apostles (Acts 1:26).

What was the purpose for the apostles receiving the Holy Spirit? The Spirit would reveal the truth (John 16:13). He would show them things to come (John 16:13). They would be taught all things, and he would bring all things to their remembrance (John 14:26).

The second case is Cornelius (Acts 10, 11, 15). Did he and his household receive Holy Spirit baptism? Peter said that the Holy Spirit was poured out on the Gentiles "also" (Acts 10:45). Two verses later he said they received the Holy Spirit "just as we have" (v. 47). That tells us that what they received was like what the apostles received. Furthermore, when Peter retold the story at Jerusalem he said the Spirit fell upon the Gentiles "as on us at the beginning" (Acts 11:15). What happened at the house of Cornelius reminded Peter of what was promised to the apostles (v. 16). Their gift of the Spirit was a "like gift" (v. 17, cf. "just as he did to us" Acts 15:8). Thus, we conclude that the household of Cornelius received Holy Spirit baptism.

What was the purpose of this? When Peter told the brethren in Jerusalem what happened, their conclusion was, "Then God has also granted to the Gentiles repentance to life" (Acts 11:18). It was to prove that the Gentiles are now gospel subjects.

2. **Those who had Holy Spirit baptism could do the following:**

   - Speak with other tongues (Acts 2:4-11; 10:46)

   - Heal the lame (Acts 3:6-11; 4:14, 16, 22)

   - Strike one dead (Acts 5:7-10)

   - Raise the dead (Acts 9:36-41; 20:9-12)

   - Strike one blind (Acts 13:7-11)

   - Speak without taking thought (Matt. 10:19)

   - Impart miraculous gifts (Acts 8:17-18)

Two purposes of Holy Spirit baptism:

- **To reveal truth to the apostles**

- **To prove that the Gentiles are gospel subjects**

3. **Today there is one baptism (Eph. 4:5).** Holy Spirit baptism and water baptism differ in a number of ways. They differ in the *element*. The element of Holy Spirit baptism is the Holy Spirit (Acts 1:5). The element of water baptism is water (Acts 8:38). They differ in the *one who administers* the baptism. Jesus baptizes with the Holy Spirit (John 1:33). Men baptize with water (Matt. 28:19). They differ in *nature*. Holy Spirit baptism is a promise (Acts 1:4-5). Water baptism is a command (Mark 16:16). They differ in their *purpose*. Holy Spirit baptism was to reveal truth (John 16:13). Water baptism is for salvation (Mark 16:16).

Since there is only one baptism today (Eph. 4:5), then which of the two has ceased? There is not a continual need to reveal truth, but there is a continual need for men to be saved. Thus, we conclude that Holy Spirit baptism has ceased.

Miracles would cease with the complete revelation.

1 Corinthians 12-14 deals with miraculous spiritual gifts. Chapter 12 deals with the *enumeration* of the gifts. Chapter 13 deals with the *duration* of those gifts. Chapter 14 deals with *regulation* of the gifts. Let's focus on the duration.

1. **The miraculous spiritual gifts would cease when the perfect came (1 Cor. 13:8-10).** Prophecies, tongues, and knowledge would fail, cease, and vanish away (v. 8). This would occur "when that which is perfect has come" (v. 10). What is "that which is perfect?"

2. **The word "perfect" means complete, rather than flawless or sinless.** Those who contend that miracles are being performed today argue that the "perfect" means flawless or sinless and thus is a reference to the second coming of Christ. Thayer's lexicon says the word means, "brought to its end, finished; wanting nothing necessary to completeness; perfect" (p. 618). W. E. Vine's dictionary says, "signifies having reached its end (*telos*), finished, complete, perfect" (Vol. III, pp. 174-175). Strong's says "complete" (#5046). Liddell and Scott say, "complete, perfect, entire" (p. 696).

The "perfect" is put in contrast to that which is "in part" (partial or incomplete). Consider how the word "perfect" is used in Matthew 5:48, which says we are to be perfect as God is. Can we be flawless or sinless? The context shows that "complete" is the idea. Just as God sends rain on the just and unjust, so we are to love those that love us and love our enemies.

3. **That which is "in part" is God's revelation, thus the "perfect" is God's revelation.** The text says, "For we know in part and we prophesy in part" (1 Cor. 13:9).

How Holy Spirit baptism and water baptism differ:

- **Element**

- **One who administers**

- **Nature**

- **Purpose**

The **"perfect"** refers to knowledge and prophecy: **God's revelation.** When God's revelation would be complete, the **miraculous gifts** would cease.

Knowledge and prophecy involved the revelation of God's will. Thus, God's revelation was referred to as being "in part" (incomplete). The perfect (complete) then refers to knowledge and prophecy: God's revelation. When God's revelation would be complete, the miraculous gifts would cease. God's word is complete (Jude 3; Jas. 1:25).

4. **The "perfect" must be of the same nature as that which is "in part."** Don't forget that the contrast is between that which is "in part" (partial or incomplete) and that which is "perfect" (complete). We know that which is "in part" is the revelation of God (1 Cor. 13:9). Thus, that which is "perfect" cannot refer to the coming of Christ. That would not make sense. Let's illustrate. I would not talk about a partially full wheelbarrow and then say, "When I get a full coffee cup I will…" As absurd as that seems, it makes as much sense as speaking of partial revelation, and then saying, "When the perfect Christ comes…"

It would make sense to speak of a partially full ice cream cone, and then say, "When I have a perfect (complete) cone, I will begin to eat it." Notice that the thing in part is of the same nature as that which is complete. Thus, our text speaks of revelation being in part (v. 9), then adds that when the complete revelation comes (v. 10) the miraculous will be done away.

5. **Two illustrations from the context help us to understand.** The first is an immature boy who grows into a mature man. Paul said, "When I was a child, I spoke as a child, I understood as a child, I thought as a child; but when I became a man, I put away childish things" (v. 11). The one immature is the same one who becomes mature. The second illustration is, "For now we see in a mirror, dimly, but then face to face. Now I know in part, but then I shall know just as I also am known" (v. 12). The same one who looks at himself in the mirror is the one who sees himself face to face.

We must conclude that 1 Corinthians 13:8-10 tells us that miraculous gifts would end when the complete revelation came.

There is no evidence of miracles today.

Those who claim to work miracles today are not doing the kind of miracles we read about in the New Testament. If anyone today has what the apostles had, they could do any one of the following.

- Speak with tongues (Acts 2:4-11; 10:46)

- Do wonders and signs (Acts 2:43)

- Heal the lame (Acts 3:6-11; 4:14, 16, 22)

- Strike one dead (Acts 5:7-10)

- Heal everyone (Acts 5:15-16)

- Raise the dead (Acts 9:36-41; 20:8-12)

- Strike one blind (Acts 13:7-11)

- Speak without taking thought (Matt. 10:19)

Is there anyone who can do all of these? In the absence of these miracles, we conclude there is no evidence of miracles today.

Questions

1. How do we know that miracles were not just for the betterment of mankind? _____
    _____
    _____

2. Give three purposes for miracles and show that the purposes have been accomplished.
    _____
    _____
    _____

3. How can we show that it was only the apostles who received Holy Spirit baptism in Acts
    2:1-4? _____
    _____
    _____

4. For what purpose did the apostles receive Holy Spirit baptism? _____
    _____
    _____

5. How would you prove that Cornelius received Holy Spirit baptism like the apostles did?
    _____
    _____

6. For what purpose did the Holy Spirit fall upon the house of Cornelius? _____
    _____
    _____

7. What is the difference in Holy Spirit baptism and water baptism? _____
    _____
    _____

8. What is the one baptism of Ephesians 4:5? _____
    _____
    _____

9. What could those who could work miracles do? _____
    _____
    _____

10. When would spiritual gifts cease? _____
    _____
    _____

11. Define "perfect" (1 Cor. 13:10). _____
    _____
    _____

12. What was "in part" (1 Cor. 13:9)? _____
    _____
    _____

13. What is the point being made in this lesson about "that which is in part must be of the
    same nature as that which is perfect?" _____
    _____
    _____
    _____

WHY WE ARE DIFFERENT
From Other Churches of Christ

Not all churches of Christ are the same. We are different in belief. We don't all believe the same thing. We differ in teaching. We don't all teach the same thing. We differ in practice since we all don't practice the same things.

At the center of those differences is respect (or the lack of it) for Bible authority. Whether the difference is over the work of the church, the organization of the church, what is to be preached, the social gospel, church recreation or divorce and remarriage, it all centers on Bible authority.

We need to be reminded of how we determine what is authorized (discussed in greater detail in lesson 9). When the issue of circumcision was raised (Acts 15), it was addressed by appealing to a command or direct statement (vv. 13-21), approved example (v. 12), and necessary inference (vv. 7-11). These principles are seen in the Lord's Supper. We observe the Lord's Supper because of a command or direct statement (1 Cor. 11:23-24). We partake on the first day of the week, and only on that day, because of an approved example (Acts 20:7). We serve it every Sunday because of necessary inference (Acts 20:7).

Thus, when we say something is not authorized, we mean that there is no command, no example and no necessary inference.

The early division in the 1800's: The church divided in 1849 over the issue of the missionary society (a separate organization between the church and the work of preaching the gospel). Ten years later (1859) the issue of instrumental music arose with the introduction of a melodeon into worship at Midway, KY. The real issue was over Bible authority. The division resulted in formation of Christian Churches and The Disciples of Christ.

The later division in the 1950's and 1960's: From around 1900 to about 1930 many orphan homes were being formed. Tennessee Orphan Home (Spring Hill, TN) was formed in 1909. Potter Orphan Home (Bowling Green, KY) was formed in 1914. Boles Home (Quinlan, TX) was formed in 1927. Tipton Home (Tipton, OK) was formed in 1928.

At the center of the **differences** in churches of Christ is **respect** (or the lack of it) for **Bible authority**.

Institutional churches of Christ: those that **support** human institutions

Non-institutional churches of Christ: those that **oppose** the support of human institutions from the **church treasury**

In the 1930's there was a greater push for putting these orphan homes in the church budget. Some who opposed the institutions later endorsed them. In the 1940's there was a renewed interest when men like N.B. Hardeman (pushing for putting the college in the church budget) shifted the issue from the college to the orphan home, saying that they stand or fall together. By the 1950's churches supporting orphan's homes were well underway. Many debates were conducted over the issue. By the 1960's the division was clear.

The real issue was over Bible authority. As a result of this division, we now have institutional churches of Christ (those that support human institutions) and non-institutional churches of Christ (those that oppose the support of human institutions from the church treasury).

The real problem was different approaches to Bible authority. One side had a "liberal" approach to the work of the church and authority. The other side had a "conservative" approach to those same things. As a result, symptoms of that problem surfaced. Those symptoms included the college in the church budget, orphan homes in the church budget, the sponsoring church arrangement, church recreation and fellowship halls.

So why are we different from other churches of Christ?

There is no authority for church support of human institutions.

1. **What is a benevolent society or orphan home?** The orphan home was a separate organization between the church and the work of benevolence. The orphans being cared for and the place where they stay is not the orphan home. The orphan homes were corporations (with a board of directors) between the church and the work being done. Churches send money to the orphan home which in turn arranges, oversees and provides for the care for orphans.

2. **What was the issue?** The issue over the orphan home was not whether orphans and others in need should be helped. It was not an issue of how the work was to be done (modes, means and methods). It was not a question of a place being maintained. Neither was it an issue of whether someone would let an orphan starve (as some charged). The issue was whether or not it is scriptural to have a separate organization between the church and the work of benevolence.

3. **The church can do its own work.** The local church can do its own work (take care of those in need) without an organization between the church and the work being done. In Acts 6:1-6 we read of widows who needed to be

taken care of at the local church expense. The congregation selected seven men to oversee this work (v.3). There was no organization set up to which they sent money. This was a simple case of the local church doing its own work.

Paul wrote, "If any believing man or woman has widows, let them relieve them, and do not let the church be burdened, that it (the church, DVR) may relieve those who are really widows" (1 Tim. 5:16). Just as the individual can "relieve" his widow without forming a separate organization, likewise the church can relieve those who are widows indeed. The church can take care of its own needy (arrange, oversee and provide for their needs).

4. **There is no command, example or necessary inference to authorize the church to send money to a human institution to care for the needy.** If so where is the passage?

There is no authority for sponsoring churches.

1. **What is a sponsoring church?** A sponsoring church is a church that takes on a work larger than it can afford (such as a large project of preaching the gospel), and several other churches send money to this "sponsoring church" so the work can be done.

2. **The *Herald of Truth* radio and television program.** One of the most notable examples of a sponsoring church is the *Herald of Truth* radio and television program that started in 1947. Four years later (1951), the Fifth and Highland church in Abilene, TX assumed the responsibility for this work. Thus, Fifth and Highland was the sponsoring church that put on the radio and TV program which featured Batsell Barrett Baxter as the speaker.

3. **What was the issue?** The issue was not a question of preaching the gospel. All agreed that should be done. It was not a question of the use of a radio or TV program. It was not a question of the good being done or whether churches could ever cooperate. It was not a matter of methods. The question was: can church "A" send money to church "B" to preach the gospel? It was an issue of whether multiple churches could work through one eldership.

4. **God's pattern must be followed.** God's pattern for *evangelism* is that a church could send a preacher out to preach the message (Acts 11:22; 13:1-ff). A church could also send money to a preacher (Phil. 4:15).

A **sponsoring church** takes on a work larger than it can **afford**, and other churches **send money** to the sponsoring church so the work can be done.

The work that God assigned the **local church** is **evangelism**, **edification**, and **benevolence**.

God's pattern is that one church can send money to another church in the work of *benevolence* (Acts 11:27-ff).

We cannot change God's pattern (Heb. 8:5) by taking his plan for *benevolence* and applying it to *evangelism*. To do so would be like taking the qualifications for elders and applying them to deacons, and vice versa.

5. **Elders' oversight is limited to the church among them (1 Pet. 5:1-3; Acts 20:28).** There is no authority for the elders of one church to oversee any part of the work of another church. The elders of the sponsoring church oversee the work that is done by thousands of churches.

6. **There is no command, example or necessary inference to authorize one church to send money to another church to preach the gospel.** If so where is the passage?

There is no authority for the social gospel.

1. **What is the social gospel?** This movement involves a great shift from the spiritual to the social. It is an effort to put the church in the business of improving the social circumstances of man. This would include the church being involved in supporting colleges, operating day care centers, sponsoring ball teams, having church kitchens and fellowship halls. Many churches have used "gimmicks" (everything from dinners and ice cream suppers to greased pig chases) to attract larger numbers in attendance.

2. **The church is not a social order.** Paul said, "the kingdom of God is not eating and drinking, but righteousness and peace and joy in the Holy Spirit" (Rom. 14:17). Jesus said, "My kingdom is not of this world. If My kingdom were of this world, My servants would fight, so that I should not be delivered to the Jews; but now My kingdom is not from here" (John 18:36). Peter emphasized that it is a spiritual kingdom, saying, "you also, as living stones, are being built up a spiritual house, a holy priesthood, to offer up spiritual sacrifices acceptable to God through Jesus Christ" (1 Peter 2:5).

3. **The gospel is not a social gospel.** When large numbers followed Jesus after feeding the five thousand, Jesus said, "Most assuredly, I say to you, you seek Me, not because you saw the signs, but because you ate of the loaves and were filled. Do not labor for the food which perishes, but for the food which endures to everlasting life…" (John 6:26-27). The gospel is a redemptive message. It is the power of God unto salvation (Rom. 1:16-17; 1 Cor. 1:18, 21; 2:2-5).

4. **The issue of eating in the church building:** The question about whether we could have meals in the church building was not a question of whether the building was sacred. It was not a question of whether one could eat inside the building or on church property. No one was contending that it was sinful to eat something on church property (i.e. preacher eating his lunch in his office or the janitor eating a snack while cleaning). The issue is: can the church have a common meal for social and recreational purposes?

5. **The work of the local church:** The work that God assigned the local church is evangelism (1 Tim. 3:15), edification (Eph. 4:16), and benevolence (1 Tim. 5:16). If one suggests that we add the work of social and recreational matters, we ask, where is the passage that authorizes such?

6. **There is no command, example or necessary inference to authorize the church to arrange and support a common meal for social and recreational purposes.** If so where is the passage?

The tolerant spirit is unscriptural.

1. **Churches must deal with sin and error in their midst.** Paul's instructions to Timothy to preach the word included reproving and rebuking (2 Tim. 4:1-5). Those who cause division and offenses contrary to the doctrine are to be marked (Rom. 16:17-18). Churches are instructed to withdraw from those who walk disorderly (1 Cor. 5:1-13; 2 Thess. 3:16-15).

2. **The tolerant spirit in some churchues of Christ:** The lack of respect for Bible authority creates a tolerant attitude toward a number of things. It is not surprising that in many churches of Christ, immodesty, dancing, social drinking, divorce and remarriage and acceptance of denominationalism goes unchecked.

3. **The spirit that is progressive allows for a complete transformation of the church.** Once respect for authority is lost, it allows for men to completely change the church until it doesn't even resemble anything we read in the Bible.

Questions

1. What is at the heart of the differences among churches of Christ? _____
   _____

2. What were the issues that divided the church in the 1800's? _____
   _____
   _____

3. What is an orphan home? _____
   _____
   _____

4. What is the real issue over orphan homes? _____
   _____
   _____

5. What is a sponsoring church? _____

_____

_____

6. What is wrong with the sponsoring church? _____

_____

_____

7. What does the limited authority of elders (overseeing the church among them) have to do with the sponsoring church issue? _____

_____

_____

8. What is the social gospel? _____

_____

_____

9. Why should the church not be involved in the social gospel? _____

_____

_____

10. What is the work of the church? _____

_____

_____

11. What are some things tolerated among some churches of Christ that should be dealt with?

_____

_____

_____

WHY WE DON'T HAVE
Church Kitchens and Fellowship Halls

It is not uncommon to find churches that have kitchens and fellowship halls (a place where they have church dinners, parties and other social gatherings). Visitors to our services will notice that we don't have such facilities. Why is that?

When we talk about a church kitchen we are not talking about a place to prepare the Lord's Supper, to wash the communion trays, or to take care of needy saints. We are talking about the church providing a place for meals for social and recreational purposes. These are sometimes called "Fellowship Halls," "Family Life Centers," or "Multi-Purpose Buildings."

Let's consider again the issue of eating in the church building. The question about whether we could have meals in the church building was not a question of whether the building was sacred. It was not a question of whether one could eat inside the building or on church property. No one was contending that it was sinful to eat something on church property (i.e. preacher eating his lunch in his office or the janitor eating a snack while cleaning). The issue is: *can the church have a common meal for social and recreational purposes?*

So, why is it that we don't have a church kitchen or a fellowship hall?

There is no Bible authority for it.

1. **How authority is determined:** We need to be reminded of how we determine what is authorized (discussed in greater detail in lesson 9). When the issue of circumcision was raised (Acts 15), it was addressed by appealing to a command or direct statement (vv. 13-21), approved example (v. 12), and necessary inference (vv. 7-11). These principles are seen in the Lord's Supper. We observe the Lord's Supper because of a command or direct statement (1 Cor. 11:23-24). We partake on the first day of the week, and only on that day, because of an approved example (Acts 20:7). We serve it every Sunday because of necessary inference (Acts 20:7).

   Thus, when we are looking for Bible authority, we are looking for a command or direct statement, an approved

There is no **command**, no **example** and no **necessary inference** to authorize the church to arrange for or support a **common meal** for social and recreational purposes.

example, or a necessary inference. There is no command, no example and no necessary inference to authorize the church to arrange for or support a common meal for social and recreational purposes. If it is authorized, where is the passage?

2. **We are looking for authority for the church to sponsor meals for social and recreational purposes.** We are not looking for a specific mention of a church kitchen or fellowship hall. If the church is authorized to have meals for social and recreational purposes, then kitchens and fellowship halls would be aids to carrying out that command.

   To illustrate, we understand aids are authorized within the command. The command to eat the Lord's Supper (1 Cor. 11) authorizes the use of plates, tables, and cups. The command to baptize (Matt. 28:19) authorizes the use of a baptistry and a heater. The command to sing (Eph. 5:19) authorizes the use of books and tuners. Those are merely aids to carrying out the command. The point here is that we are not looking for a passage that mentions a kitchen or a fellowship hall. What we are looking for is a passage that authorizes the church to have meals for social and recreational purposes.

It is not the work of the church.

1. **The work of the church is three-fold.** First, the church is commissioned to be engaged in *evangelism*. The church is the pillar and ground of truth (1 Tim. 3:15). Second, the church is to *edify* (build up spiritually) itself (Eph. 4:16). Edification comes through the revelation of God (1 Cor. 14:1-5; Rom. 10:17). Third, in *benevolence*, the church is to take care of its own needy saints (1 Tim. 5:16).

   If we want to add another work for the church (social and recreational activities), where is the passage that authorizes the church to do that work?

A **church kitchen** is not a part of **evangelism**, **edification** of the saints, or **benevolence** to needy saints.

2. **A church kitchen is not the work of the church.** A church kitchen (or fellowship hall) is not a part of the work of evangelism. Some have thought that churches could attract numbers by offering food, and then teach them the gospel. Nothing of the kind was done in the New Testament. If it takes a biscuit or burger to bring them, it will take a biscuit or burger to keep them. A church kitchen is not a part of the work of edification. A church kitchen is not a part of the work of benevolence. If we want to add another work for the church (social and recreational activities), where is the passage that authorizes the church to do that work?

The church is not a social order; the gospel is not a social gospel.

Let's consider two points from our previous lesson and then add some additional thoughts.

1. **The church is not a social order.** Paul said, "the kingdom of God is not eating and drinking, but righteousness and peace and joy in the Holy Spirit" (Rom. 14:17). Jesus said, "My kingdom is not of this world. If My kingdom were of this world, My servants would fight, so that I should not be delivered to the Jews; but now My kingdom is not from here" (John 18:36). Peter said the church is a spiritual house (1 Peter 2:5).

2. **The gospel is not a social gospel.** When large numbers followed Jesus after feeding the five thousand, "Jesus answered them and said, 'Most assuredly, I say to you, you seek Me, not because you saw the signs, but because you ate of the loaves and were filled. Do not labor for the food which perishes, but for the food which endures to everlasting life…'" (John 6:26-27).

3. **The gospel is a redemptive message.** The great commission shows that the gospel to be preached to the world concerned salvation from sin (Mark 16:15-16; Luke 24:47). God's plan for making men righteous is found in the gospel (Rom. 1:16-17). The gospel is God's message to save (1 Cor. 1:18, 21). We are saved by the gospel (1 Cor. 15:1-3). Every gospel sermon found in the book of Acts focused on salvation.

   The gospel does not address the social ills of society, but it is a message of redemption.

Individual liberties and responsibilities are not church liberties and responsibilities.

1. **The issues of 1950's and 1960's made two major shifts.** First, there was a shift from the spiritual to the social. The church sponsored human institutions (lesson 11) involved that shift. Then later when church kitchens and fellowship halls were introduced, the shift was being made again. The second shift was from the individual to the church. Liberties and responsibilities of the individual have been pushed on to the church.

2. **There is a difference in the individual and the church.** Paul's instructions in 1 Timothy 5:16 well illustrate the difference. Here the individual is charged to take care of his

The **gospel** does not address the **social ills** of society, but it is a message of **redemption**.

Paul's answer to the problem of the Corinthians making a **common meal** of the Lord's Supper, was not to make sure it was in the **fellowship hall**, but to have it in their own **houses**.

widow, and the church is not to be burdened with it. Clearly, the individual has a responsibility that the church does not.

3. **The individual and the church differ in name.**
   The individual wears the name "Christian" (Acts 11:26; 1 Pet. 4:16). The church is never called "Christian." The church is referred to as a "church of Christ" (Rom. 16:16) or "church of God" (1 Cor. 1:2).

4. **The individual and the church differ in work.**
   The individual takes care of his own widow while the church takes care of the widows indeed (1 Tim. 5:16).

5. **The individual and the church differ in finances.**
   The individual can buy and sell to gain money (Jas. 4:13). However, there is no authority for the church to do so. The church gets its money through free will offerings (1 Cor. 16:1-2).

6. **Common meals are individual matters.** Paul said, "When ye come together therefore into one place, this is not to eat the Lord's supper. For in eating every one taketh before other his own supper: and one is hungry, and another is drunken. What? *have ye not houses to eat and to drink in?* or despise ye the church of God, and shame them that have not? What shall I say to you? shall I praise you in this? I praise you not" (1 Cor. 11:20-22; emphasis mine, DVR). Paul's answer to the problem of the Corinthians making a common meal of the Lord's Supper, was not to make sure it was in the fellowship hall, but to have it in their own houses.

7. **There is a difference in incidental matters while at the building and something planned and sponsored by the church.** We might have conversations with one another over politics. But that does not mean that the church can plan and organize a political rally. We might talk to some member about buying something from them. But that does not mean that the church can set up a business. While at services, one might seek medical advice from a nurse or doctor who is a member. But that does not mean the church can set up a hospital or clinic. The same is true when it comes to eating. We may eat while on church property (preacher eats his lunch in his office, the cleaning person brings a snack while cleaning, etc.). But that doesn't mean that the church is authorized to have a church kitchen or serve a common meal.

Questions

1. What is the real issue about eating in the church building? _____

    _____

    _____

2. How do we establish Bible authority? (Use Acts 15 to show your answer). _____

    _____

    _____

3. When asking for authority for church kitchens and fellowship halls, what are we looking for if it is not a kitchen or fellowship hall specifically mentioned in the text? _____

    _____

    _____

4. What is the work of the church? _____

    _____

    _____

5. Under what kind of work does a church kitchen and fellowship hall come? _____

    _____

    _____

6. What does it mean that the gospel is a "redemptive message?" _____

    _____

    _____

7. What are the two major shifts that took place in the issues that divided churches of Christ?

    _____

    _____

8. How does 1 Timothy 5:16 demonstrate a difference in the individual and the church? ____

    _____

    _____

9. In what ways are the individual and the church different? _____

    _____

    _____

10. How would you show that common meals are individual matters? _____

    _____

    _____

WHY WE DON'T HAVE
Women Preachers

Some churches have women preachers. As women have taken on roles of leadership in the business and political world, the same has been true in religious circles.

We are not talking about women teaching other women. We are not talking about women teaching children. We are talking about women publicly preaching to mixed audiences (men and women).

We do not oppose women preachers because we don't like women. I know of no one among churches of Christ who dislikes women. We do not oppose them because we think women cannot do as well as men. They could. We do not object to women preachers because we think women are inferior. They are not. It is not because we think women don't know their Bibles. In many cases, women know their Bibles better than men. Neither is it because we want to hold to old traditions.

Let's consider that men and women are equal. Paul wrote, "There is neither Jew nor Greek, there is neither slave nor free, there is neither male nor female; for you are all one in Christ Jesus" (Gal. 3:28). Being equal does not mean they have the same roles or place of authority.

So why do we oppose women preaching?

God placed man (not woman) in leadership.

1. **Generally (1 Cor. 11:1-3):** The text says, "Imitate me, just as I also imitate Christ. Now I praise you, brethren, that you remember me in all things and keep the traditions just as I delivered them to you. But I want you to know that the head of every man is Christ, the head of woman is man, and the head of Christ is God." The order of authority given in this text is, God, Christ, man, and woman. Thus, man is in leadership over the woman.

2. **In the home (Eph. 5:22-24; 1 Pet. 3:1-7):** God made the husband the head of the wife. The wife is to submit to the leadership of her husband. Thus, man is in leadership over the woman.

> Being **equal** does not mean men and women have the **same roles** or place of **authority**.

2. **In the church (men are to lead):** Elders (who oversee the congregation) are men (1 Tim. 3:1-7; Titus 1:5-9). Deacons are men (1 Tim.3:8-13). Preachers were men. Peter and the other apostles who preached in Acts 2 and again in the next chapter were men. Paul (whose sermons are recorded in Acts 13, 17) was a man. Stephen (Acts 6-7) and Philip (Acts 8) were men.

Since man has been placed in leadership, women can't take on a leadership role in preaching.

Women are not to teach over a man.

Paul wrote, "Let a woman learn in silence with all submission. And I do not permit a woman to teach or to have authority over a man, but to be in silence. For Adam was formed first, then Eve. And Adam was not deceived, but the woman being deceived, fell into transgression" (1 Tim. 2:11-14).

1. **The context:** The surrounding verses discuss the role of men and women. Men (*aner*—males only) are to pray everywhere (v. 8). Since this is males only, it must refer to men leading in public worship (cf. 1 Cor. 14:16). Women are to live in submission (vv. 9-14).

2. **The restriction (v. 12):** A woman is not to teach over a man. A woman is not to have authority over a man. The expression, "over a man" qualifies both "not to teach" and "not to have authority." A woman can teach, but not over a man. When a woman preaches she violates these restrictions. She is teaching over a man. She is having authority over a man.

3. **The reasons (vv. 13-14):** Two reasons are given for these restrictions. First, the order of creation—Adam was formed first (cf. Gen. 2:22-24). The second, the matter of the transgression—the woman was deceived (cf. Gen. 3:1-6, 16).

Some (the "Biblical feminist") contend that the restrictions of Paul were based on the culture of the time. As culture changes, so do the restrictions. However, these reasons given in our text do not change. The order of creation is still the same. The matter of Eve's transgression has not changed.

Since a woman cannot teach over a man and cannot have authority over a man, she cannot preach.

Women are not to address the assembly.

In his letter to the Corinthians, Paul wrote, "Let your women keep silent in the churches, for they are not permitted to speak; but they are to be submissive, as the law also says. And if they want to learn something, let them ask their own husbands at home; for it is shameful for women to speak in church" (1 Cor. 14:34-35).

> The **reasons** given for the submission of women **do not change**. The order of **creation** and the matter of **Eve's transgression** are still the same.

Here we learn that women are to keep silent in the church. To understand, we need to clarify "silent" and "church."

1. **The context:** The term "church" in this context refers to the assembly. Just a few verses earlier the apostle wrote, "Therefore if the whole church *comes together in one place,* and all speak with tongues, and there come in those who are uninformed or unbelievers, will they not say that you are out of your mind?" (v. 23; emphasis mine, DVR). When the church comes together in one place, that is the assembly.

2. **Silent (v. 34):** What is meant by "silent?" She must be silent in the sense of the context. She must sing in the assembly as commanded of all Christians (Eph.5:19; Col. 3:16). When she sings she is not violating the command to be silent. Her silence is defined, "for they are not permitted to speak; but they are to be submissive…" (1 Cor. 14:34). She is not to speak in any way that is out of her role of submission to man. She is not to speak in any way that is over a man. She is not to address the assembly.

If women cannot address the assembly, they cannot preach.

What can a woman do?

If a woman cannot teach over a man, have authority over a man or address the assembly, then what can she do?

1. **She can teach women and children.** The restrictions on women do not mean she cannot do any teaching at all. Older women are to teach younger women (Titus 2:3-4). Paul told Timothy to teach men (*anthropos*—mankind) who would teach even others (2 Tim. 2:2). The word "men" does not mean males only (as *aner* does; 1 Tim. 2:8), but includes men and women (mankind). Thayer's Lexicon says, "with refer to sex (contextually)."

2. **She can serve in some special way (Rom. 16:1).** Phoebe was a "servant" of the church at Cenchrea. She may do some task the elders request. She could handle correspondence for them. She may talk to another sister about a problem the elders want her to address (that might be handled better by a woman).

3. **She may humbly correct a man (Acts 18:24-28).** Aquila and Priscilla both were involved in correcting Apollos in his error. Whatever role Priscilla played it did not violate the restrictions we have noticed above (1 Tim. 2:11-12; 1 Cor. 14:34-35).

4. **She may ask or answer questions in a class.** When she does so, she is not addressing the assembly (the church is not all in one place). She would not be teaching or having authority over a man.

5. **She can do anything that does not violate her limitations.**

A woman must **sing** in the assembly, as commanded of **all Christians**. She is not violating the command to be **silent**.

Questions

1. In what way(s) are men and women equal?_____
    _____
    _____

2. What is the order of headship (1 Cor. 11:1-3) and where does that apply? _____
    _____
    _____

3. How does man being in leadership address the question of women being preachers?
    _____
    _____

4. What restrictions are placed on women in 1 Timothy 2:11-12? _____
    _____
    _____

5. How do we know that 1 Timothy 2:11-12 does not forbid a woman to teach?_____
    _____
    _____

6. What reasons are given in the context of 1 Timothy 2 for the restrictions on women?
    _____
    _____

7. How would you answer the contention that the restrictions found in 1 Timothy 2 were
    based on culture? _____
    _____
    _____

8. What does "church" mean in 1 Corinthians 14:34-35? _____
    _____
    _____

9. In what sense is a woman to be "silent" (1 Corinthians 14:34-35)? _____
    _____
    _____

10. Give evidence that a woman can teach women and children. _____
    _____
    _____

11. List some ways a woman could be a special servant (Rom. 16:1). _____
    _____
    _____

WHY WE
Withdraw from the Unfaithful

When a member of the church becomes unfaithful and persists in that sin, the church withdraws from him. We do not withdraw the first moment he sins. Action to withdraw comes only after it is evident that the person is not repenting. Several attempts are usually made to talk with the person and plead for repentance. In time, we communicate to the person (often by letter) telling them that we will withdraw from them at a set time (in a week or two). Then, a statement is made before the congregation that we are withdrawing from the brother or sister who persists in sin. From that point on, other members do not socialize with that person (in an effort to bring them to repentance).

When this is done, questions and charges are often made. Someone will charge that we are kicking them out of the church. Such is not so. The questions will be raised, "How could you mistreat people this way?" Others will urge that we should have shown love and concern instead of withdrawing. Some even get the idea in their head that we are asking them not to even attend services. "This is mean and hateful," someone will be sure to say. All such charges are based on a misunderstanding of what withdrawing is.

Two main passages on withdrawing

1 Corinthians 5: The entire chapter is devoted to a discussion of the need for church discipline at Corinth.

1. **The situation (vv. 1-2):** There was a fornicator in the church that had not repented of his sin. The church had done little or nothing about it. Thus, Paul addresses their need to withdraw from him.

2. **The instruction (vv. 3-13):** The divine instruction was to put him away from among them (vv. 3-4, 13). The purpose is two-fold (vv. 5-8). First, this is to save the brother who is guilty (v. 5). Secondly, this is to keep the church pure (vv. 6-8). The instructions included not to keep company with the one who is disciplined (vv. 9-13). The word *company* literally means "to mix up together with"—a description of socializing. That is to be withheld in an effort to bring him to repentance.

The **purpose** of withdrawing is two-fold: to **save** the one who is guilty and to keep the church **pure**.

> When the church at Corinth **finally acted**, it brought the brother to **repentance**.

3. **The conclusion:** From this chapter we have to conclude the following: Ignoring the unfaithful is wrong. Doing nothing about the sinner doesn't please God or save the sinner. Withdrawing is an effort to save. Does it work? When the church at Corinth finally acted, it brought the brother to repentance (2 Cor. 2).

2 Thessalonians 3:6-15: This chapter concerns a problem with some unfaithful at Thessalonica.

1. **The situation (vv. 7-13):** Some had taught a doctrine that the second coming of Christ was imminent (about to happen). Thus, some had quit working (vv.7-12) and become busybodies (vv. 11-12). This behavior was described as walking disorderly (v. 6).

2. **The instruction (vv. 6, 14-15):** The divine instruction was to withdraw from those who walk disorderly (v. 6). To do so, the person must be identified (v. 14). Part of carrying out the instructions included not keeping company with the one who is being disciplined (v. 14). Their dealing with the brother was not to be as an enemy, but treated as a brother whom they are admonishing to do better (v. 15).

3. **The conclusion:** From this chapter we must conclude that withdrawing is a command. When we withdraw it is an effort to bring them to repentance (v. 14). When such action is taken, this is not mistreatment or being some kind of an enemy.

   With these two passages as a basis for answering our question, let's consider three basic reasons why we withdraw from the unfaithful.

Because the authority of Christ says to

1. **We are under the authority of Christ.** Christ has all authority (Matt. 28:18-19). We must abide by the authority of Christ (Col. 3:17). Thus, we are obliged to withdraw from the unfaithful since Christ commands us to.

2. **Specifically in the texts:** Both texts specifically mention the authority of Christ in connection with the instructions to withdraw. Paul wrote to the Corinthians, "*In the name of the Lord Jesus Christ*, when you are gathered together, along with my spirit, with the power of our Lord Jesus Christ, deliver such a one to Satan for the destruction of the flesh, that his spirit may be saved in the day of the Lord Jesus" (1 Cor. 5:4-5; emphasis mine, DVR). The instructions to the Thessalonians said, "But we command you, brethren, *in the name of our Lord Jesus Christ*, that you withdraw from every brother who

walks disorderly and not according to the tradition which he received from us" (2 Thess. 3:6; emphasis mine, DVR).

We withdraw from the unfaithful to obey Christ, whether or not we see anything else accomplished!

To bring the unfaithful to repentance

1. **The goal should always be to restore the erring (Jas. 5:19-20; Gal. 6:1).** Rather than ignore the erring, we should show love and concern by encouraging them to change (cf. 1 Cor. 5:2).

2. **Withdrawing is designed to produce repentance.** The brother at Corinth was to be dealt with "that his spirit may be saved in the day of the Lord Jesus" (1 Cor. 5:5). Those at Thessalonica were to be withdrawn from so that they might be ashamed (2 Thess. 3:14).

3. **It works (2 Cor. 2).** Quite often someone will ask if we know of a case when withdrawing ever brought a person back to the Lord. Sure we do—the fornicator at Corinth (among a number of cases in our own time). The church had taken the action that Paul had instructed (1 Cor. 5). Paul later wrote, "This punishment which was inflicted by the majority is sufficient for such a man, so that, on the contrary, you ought rather to forgive and comfort him, lest perhaps such a one be swallowed up with too much sorrow. Therefore I urge you to reaffirm your love to him" (2 Cor. 2:6-8).

4. **How it works:** When we withdraw from a brother it brings him to shame (2 Thess. 3:14). It causes him to think about his sin. When other brethren refuse to socialize with him, he comes to realize that something is missing (1 Cor. 5:9-13; 2 Thess. 3:14). That is by design. This is to help the brother come to repentance.

   One reason church discipline doesn't work more often is that we defeat it from the start by not withholding the socializing. We reason that it doesn't apply to family or close friends and thus continue to have a social relation with the brother, thinking we are helping him. Here, the very people who could bring him to shame (by not keeping company) are hindering the process.

To keep the church pure

1. **God wants the church to be pure.** Paul wrote, "that He might sanctify and cleanse her with the washing of water by the word, that He might present her to Himself a glorious

> The **very people** who could bring him to **shame** (family or close friends) are **hindering** the process.

church, not having spot or wrinkle or any such thing, but that she should be holy and without blemish" (Eph. 5:26-27).

2. **If sin is not corrected, it corrupts the whole church.** The Corinthians were warned that "a little leaven leavens the whole lump" (1 Cor. 5:6). When sin goes unchecked, others may begin to do the same. To say the least, when another is guilty of the same sin it is difficult to encourage him to repent when others are doing the same and nothing is being done.

3. **Withdrawing takes away the unfaithful.** After the above warning Paul wrote, "Therefore purge out the old leaven, that you may be a new lump, since you truly are unleavened. For indeed Christ, our Passover, was sacrificed for us" (1 Cor. 5:7). By identifying and withdrawing from the one who persists in sin, the purity of the church is maintained. Paul closed his instructions to the Corinthians by saying, "put away from yourselves the evil person" (v. 13).

4. **It causes others to fear.** When others see that sin is not being tolerated, it makes them realize their sin will be dealt with too. When they see that those who continue in sin are no longer a part of the group that the faithful keep company with (1 Cor. 5:9-13), they will think twice about their own sin. Though not a case of withdrawing, the situation with Ananias and Sapphira (Acts 5) lying about their contribution and suffering death as a consequence illustrates our point. When others saw that they didn't get away with their sin, the text says, "So great fear came upon all the church and upon all who heard these things" (v. 11).

Conclusion

We withdraw from the unfaithful to obey Christ, to restore the erring, and to keep the church pure.

Questions

1. What are some misconceptions that people have about withdrawing? _____
    _____
    _____

2. What was the situation at Corinth (1 Cor. 5)? _____
    _____
    _____

3. What was the situation at Thessalonica (2 Thess. 3)?_____
    _____
    _____

4. What instructions were given to the Corinthians (1 Cor. 5:3-13)? _____
    _____
    _____

5. What instructions were given to the Thessalonians (2 Thess. 3:6-15)? _____
    _____
    _____

6. What is the two-fold purpose of withdrawing as described in 1 Corinthians 5:5-8? _____
    _____
    _____

7. How does withdrawing bring one to repentance? _____
    _____
    _____

8. How does withdrawing maintain the purity of the church? _____
    _____
    _____

9. What does "a little leaven leavens the whole lump" (1 Cor. 5:6) mean? _____
    _____
    _____

10. For class discussion: To whom does the prohibition "not to keep company" apply? Does it
    apply to family and close friends? When this is not practiced, does that defeat our effort to
    reach the erring? _____
    _____
    _____

WHY WE DON'T HAVE
A Christmas Program

Many churches have Christmas programs. Plays depicting the Christmas story and manger scenes are common. Many songs about the birth of Jesus will be sung. Church buildings will be decorated with Christmas trees, garland and wreaths. Some will have parties with fun, food and gifts.

Why do we not have such Christmas programs?[1]

We are not told when Jesus was born.

1. **We don't know the year Jesus was born.** He was born somewhere between 7 BC and 4 BC. The problem was the calendar. Henry Halley wrote in a section he called "Why Christ was born 4 years 'Before Christ'":

   When Christ was born, time was reckoned in the Roman Empire from the founding of the city of Rome. When Christianity became the universal religion over what had been the Roman world, a monk named Dionysius Exiguus, at the request of the Emperor Justinian, made a calendar, 526 AD, reckoning time from the Birth of Christ, to supersede the Roman calendar. Long after the Christian calendar had replaced the Roman calendar, it was found that Dionysius had made a mistake in placing the birth of Christ in year 753 A U C. (From the founding of Rome). It should have been 749 or a year or two earlier. So the reason we say that Christ was born in 4 BC is merely because the maker of the Christian calendar made a mistake of 4 or 5 years in coordinating it with the Roman calendar which it replaced (*Halleys Bible Handbook*, 436).

2. **We don't know the month or the day Jesus was born.** The Bible doesn't say. It most likely was not on December 25. Luke's record says, "Now there were in the same country shepherds living out in the fields, keeping watch over their flock by night" (2:8). It would not be likely that the shepherds would be in the field in December.

   The climate was mild, and, to keep their flocks from straying, they spent the night with them. It is also a fact that the Jews sent out

Jesus was born somewhere between **7 BC** and **4 BC**. The maker of the Christian calendar made a mistake of **4 or 5 years** in coordinating it with the Roman calendar which it **replaced**.

[1] This material leans heavily on Ferrell Jenkins' material on Christmas (www.bibleworld.com/Xmas05.pdf; www.cvillechurch.com/Articles2007/Article_Christmas.htm)

The **legendary** date of **December 25** cannot be traced back farther than the **fourth century**.

their flocks into the mountainous and desert regions during the summer months, and took them up in the latter part of October or the first of November, when the cold weather commenced. While away in these deserts and mountainous regions, it was proper that there should be someone to attend them to keep them from straying and from the ravages of wolves and other wild beasts. It is probable from this that our Saviour was born before the 25th of December, or before what we call "Christmas." At that time it is cold, and especially in the high and mountainous regions about Bethlehem. But the exact time of his birth is unknown; there is no way to ascertain it. By different learned men it has been fixed at each month in the year. Nor is it of consequence to "know" the time; if it were, God would have preserved the record of it. Matters of moment are clearly revealed; those which "he" regards as of no importance are concealed (Albert Barnes, *Barnes Notes*, Comments on Luke 2:8).

The exact date of Jesus' birth is unknown; the legendary date of December 25 cannot be traced back farther than the fourth century (*The Wycliffe Bible Commentary*).

It was a custom among the Jews to send out their sheep to the deserts, about the Passover, and bring them home at the commencement of the first rain: during the time they were out, the shepherds watched them night and day. As the Passover occurred in the spring, and the first rain began early in the month of Marchesvan, which answers to part of our October and November, we find that the sheep were kept out in the open country during the whole of the summer. And as these shepherds had not yet brought home their flocks, it is a presumptive argument that October had not yet commenced, and that, consequently, our Lord was not born on the 25th of December, when no flocks were out in the fields; nor could he have been born later than September, as the flocks were still in the fields by night. On this very ground the nativity in December should be given up. The feeding of the flocks by night in the fields is a chronological fact, which casts considerable light upon this disputed point (*Adam Clarke's Commentary*).

The observance of Christmas is not of divine appointment, nor is it of New Testament origin. The day of Christ's birth cannot be ascertained from the New Testament, or indeed, from any other source. The (church) fathers of the first three centuries do not speak of any special observance of the nativity (birth) of Christ...The institution may be sufficiently explained by the circumstance that it was the taste of the age to multiply festivals...at the same time the heathen winter holidays (Saturnalia, Juvenalia Brumalia) were undoubtedly transformed, and, so to speak, sanctified by the establishment of the Christian cycle of holidays; and the heathen customs...were brought over into Christian use (*The Cyclopedia of Ecclesiastical Literature by McClintock and Strong*, Vol.2, p.276).

In spite of all this, there are some who suggest that a December birthdate is possible.

> But recent travelers tell us that in the end of December, after the rains, the flowers come again into bloom, and the flocks again issue forth. The nature of the seasons in Palestine could hardly have been unknown to those who fixed upon the present Christmas-period: the difficulty, therefore, is perhaps more imaginary than real (*Jamieson, Fausset, and Brown Commentary*).

If December is the birth of Christ, it is a pure guess!

Many dates have been suggested for the birth of Christ: January 6, March 25, January 10, May 20, and December 25. In fact, every month in the year has been suggested at some point.

3. **What we do know about the birth of Christ.** We know only what we find written in the text. The birth of Jesus was in Bethlehem (Matt. 1:25; Luke 2:1-7). The shepherds visited the same night (Luke 2:8-20). Jesus was circumcised the eighth day (Luke 2:21). Jesus' presentation was forty days after his birth (Luke 2:22; Lev. 12:2-6). The wise men visited (Matt. 2:1-12). We are not told how many wise men there were. They came to the house, not the manger (Matt. 2:11). Jesus' parents journeyed (taking him) to Egypt (Matt. 2:13-15). The male children were killed in an unsuccessful effort to kill Jesus (Matt. 2:16-18). They then returned to Nazareth (Luke 2:39; Matt. 2:19-23).

4. **How did December 25 become the birth of Christ? It is not because of the Bible.** There is no record in the Bible of Jesus being born on December 25. "Christmas was not among the earliest festivals of the church" (*Catholic Ency.* Vol. 3, 724).

Origen (245) repudiated the idea of keeping the birthday of Christ as if he were a king Pharaoh (*Encyclopedia Britannica*, 1975, Vol. 5, 642). Clement of Alexandria. (c. 200) mentioned several speculations on the date of Christ's birth and condemned them as superstitious (*ibid.*).

There is a pagan background to December 25. "The Christmas date, December 25, is first met with in the West in the 4th century (the eastern date was January 6), and was then possibly borrowed from a pagan festival." (ISBE, 3:1628). The Roman Saturnalia was a seven day Pagan Festival (Dec. 17-24) in honor of Saturn. The 25th was a day of worship of Sun-God, Mathra. This was a celebration of victory of light over darkness.

The *Encyclopedia Britannica* reports that "the traditional customs connected with Christmas have developed from several sources as a result of the coincidence of the celebration of the birth of Christ with the pagan agricultural and solar observations at midwinter. In the Roman world the Saturnalia

The **traditional customs** connected with Christmas have developed as a result of the **coincidence** of the celebration of the birth of Christ with the **pagan** agricultural and solar observations at **midwinter**.

(December 17) was a time of merrymaking and exchange of gifts. December 25 was also regarded as the birth date of the Iranian mystery god Mithra, the Sun of Righteousness."

There is a Catholic background to December 25. Liberius, Bishop of Rome (Pope), changed the date from January 6 (in 353) to December 25 (in 354). He arrived at date saying that conception was March 25 and then added 9 months.

> Despite the beliefs about Christ that the birth stories expressed, the church did not observe a festival for the celebration of the event until the 4th century. The date was chosen to counter the pagan festivities connected with the winter solstice; since 274, under the emperor Aurelian, Rome had celebrated the feast of the 'Invincible Sun' on December 25 (*Grolier Interactive*).

> After the triumph of Constantine, the church at Rome assigned December 25 as the date for the celebration of the feast, possibly about A.D. 320 or 353. By the end of the fourth century the whole Christian world was celebrating Christmas on that day, with the exception of the Eastern churches, where it was celebrated on January 6. The choice of December 25 was probably influenced by the fact that on this day the Romans celebrated the Mithraic feast of the Sun-god (*natalis solis invicti*), and that the Saturnalia also came at this time (*Colliers Encyclopedia*).

We are not authorized to observe His birth.

1. **There is no Bible authority.** Observing the birth of Christ is a religious act. We must have Bible authority for all that we do in religion (Col. 3:17; 2 John 9). There is no authority for observing the birth of Christ. There is no command, example or necessary inference to authorize such an observance.

2. **We are forbidden to observe special days (Gal. 4:8-10).** "We should observe as seasons of holy time what it can be proved God has commanded us, and no more" (Albert Barnes).

3. **Why do what is not authorized and fail to do what is authorized?** Some will only attend church services at Christmas or Easter. Yet, they fail to observe his death every Lord's day, which is authorized (Acts 20:7).

A Christmas program is entertainment.

1. **A Christmas program is presented to entertain.** The plays, skits, songs, manger scenes, etc. are presented to entertain.

2. **Entertainment is not a work of the church.** Entertainment is not worship (John 4:24). Entertainment is not evangelism (1 Tim. 3:15). Entertainment is not edification (Eph. 4:16). Entertainment is not benevolence (1 Tim. 5:16). Thus, entertainment is not authorized as a work of the church.

Some will **only** attend church services at **Christmas** or **Easter**. Yet, they fail to observe his death **every Lord's day**, which is authorized.

Questions

1. List some ways you know that churches celebrate Christmas. _____
    _____
    _____

2. Why do we not know the year that Jesus was born? _____
    _____
    _____

3. How does Luke 2:8 help us in determining whether December 25 is the birth of Christ?
    _____
    _____

4. What other dates (besides Dec. 25) have been suggested for the birth of Christ? _____
    _____
    _____

5. How does December 25 being chosen as the birth of Christ have a pagan background?
    _____
    _____

6. How does December 25 being chosen as the birth of Christ have a Catholic background?
    _____
    _____

7. What does Bible authority have to do with the question of celebrating Christmas as the
    birth of Christ? _____
    _____
    _____

8. Explain how Galatians 4:8-10 (observing days) addresses the question of celebrating
    Christmas in a religious way. _____
    _____
    _____

9. What is wrong with the church being involved in entertainment? _____
    _____
    _____

10. How would you answer the argument that says you are not very religious or excited about
    Christ if you don't celebrate his birth? _____
    _____
    _____

WHY WE BELIEVE
Jesus Was Raised from the Dead

The resurrection of Jesus Christ is at the heart and core of all that we believe. If Jesus was raised from the dead, we must conclude there is a God. How else could he have been raised? Thus, the resurrection of Christ proves that God exists. If Jesus was raised from the dead, Jesus is indeed the Son of God (Rom. 1:4). If Jesus was raised from the dead, the word of God is true.

The resurrection of Christ is the "hub" of the gospel. All that Christianity involves revolves around that "hub." Paul argues in 1 Corinthians 15:14-18 that if Christ is not raised, preaching is vain, faith is vain, the apostles are false witnesses, and we all are still in sin. Our faith, our salvation, and our hope all center on the resurrection of Christ.

What evidence can be given that Jesus was indeed raised from the dead?

Our **faith**, our **salvation**, and our **hope** all center on the **resurrection of Christ**.

The empty tomb

1. **It is a fact that the tomb is empty.** When the two Marys arrived at the tomb and found the stone rolled away, the angel said, "Come, see the place where the Lord lay" (Matt. 28:6). Luke's account says they "found not the body of the Lord Jesus" (Luke 24:3). The fact that the tomb was empty was admitted by the enemies as well (Matt. 28:11-15).

2. **How did the tomb become empty?** Those who deny the resurrection suggest three theories for the disappearance of the body of Jesus.

   The "Swoon Theory": This concept says that Jesus really didn't die but merely fainted. After being placed in the tomb, he came to himself and escaped. If he didn't really die, he still could not escape from the tomb. Don't forget the great stone placed at the only entrance (or exit) of the tomb. If three women couldn't move the stone (Mark 16:3) then neither could Jesus in His weakened condition. Remember that he had nails driven through his hands and feet. His side had been pierced causing blood and water to flow forth. He hadn't eaten in three days.

Those who were there knew that he had died. Both the disciples and the enemies admitted that He was dead.

The disciples stole the body. This was the charge made. "His disciples came by night, and stole him away while we slept" (Matt. 28:13). However, we read a little further that they were bribed (v. 15). It is interesting to note that they said that it happened while they slept. No one is competent to testify of what took place while he was asleep. The disciples would have to have done this in the face of the guards that watched. They would have to have enough men to move the great stone. Do you think they could have done all that without waking the guards, granting they were asleep?

If the disciples had the body of Jesus, they wouldn't dare make claims that it was alive. The Roman authorities would make them produce the body. If they had the dead body they would have kept their mouths shut. Hence, it is obvious that the disciples didn't take the body.

Enemies stole it. If that were so, they would have produced the dead body to disprove the resurrection. Consider what they could have done to Christianity on the day of Pentecost while Peter preached about the resurrection (Acts 2:24-36) if they had the dead body. All they would have to do to destroy the religion of Christ was to produce the dead body.

What motive would these have for taking the body? Proof for them would still be in the tomb. By taking the body they would only cause others to believe in the resurrection. If they had it, the disciples surely wouldn't make claims that it was alive.

Really was raised. The only alternative then is that there must have been a bodily resurrection from the dead. If Christ couldn't escape by His own physical strength, the disciples didn't steal the body, and the enemies didn't get it, then the only conclusion is that God raised him from the dead! That was the conclusion of the angel (Matt. 28:7). Furthermore, it fulfilled prophecy (Psa. 16:10).

Transformation of the disciples

1. **When Jesus died, the disciples were in utter despair.** However, shortly after the resurrection, their hope was restored. What caused the change? A simple removal of the body from the tomb wouldn't. The only thing that could change these disciples would be if they saw Jesus alive. Keep in mind that they were not expecting a resurrection (Luke 24:11).

If Christ couldn't **escape** by His own physical strength, the disciples **didn't steal** the body, and the **enemies** didn't get it, then the only conclusion is that **God raised him** from the dead!

2. **Let's take Peter as an example.** Just prior to the death of Jesus, Peter denied the Lord, cursing and swearing (Matt. 26:69-75). At the tomb, when he saw that the body of Jesus was missing and the linen clothes, he was "wondering in himself at that which was come to pass" (Luke 24:12). However, just a few days later he was a changed man. We find him boldly proclaiming, "Be it known unto you all, and to all the people of Israel, that by the name of Jesus Christ of Nazareth whom ye crucified, whom God raised from the dead, even by him doth this man stand before you whole" (Acts 4:10). When he was threatened for teaching what he did, he said, "Whether it be right in the sight of God to hearken unto you more than unto God, judge ye. For we cannot but speak the things we have seen and heard" (vv. 19-20). This doesn't sound like the same man we read about in Matthew 26 or Luke 24. Something changed the man. What was it? Nothing but the resurrected Lord could do that.

> Just prior to the death of Jesus, Peter **denied the Lord**, cursing and swearing. A few days later he was a **changed man**.

Change in the Jews

1. **The Jews wanted to kill Jesus.** At his trial they shouted "crucify him" (Mark 8:13, 14). These were some of the very ones that were present on Pentecost whom Peter said had crucified Jesus (Acts 2:22-23).

2. **What they heard (Acts 2):** Those present on Pentecost heard a sermon about the resurrection of Christ (vv. 24-36). Peter shows that when Christ was raised, it fulfilled prophecy (Psa. 16:10). He further demonstrated that the Psalm could not refer to David. He concluded that Jesus is now alive and is both Lord and Christ (v. 36).

3. **They changed!** When they heard the message about the resurrection, they were pricked in their hearts and asked what they must do (Acts 2:37). They were told to repent and be baptized in the name (submitting to the authority) of Christ (v. 38). They did what they were told (v. 41). They were convinced of a bodily resurrection of Christ!

Witnesses

There were many who saw the resurrected Lord and testified about it.

1. **Criteria for credible witnesses:** How do we know they were true witnesses? Simon Greenleaf, author of *Testimony of the Evangelist*, practiced law from 1806 to 1853. He was a professor at Harvard. Greenleaf became a respected authority on witnesses. He said, "The credit due to the testimony of witnesses depends upon, firstly, their honesty;

Do you think the disciples would **suffer** for something they **knew** to be a lie?

secondly, their ability; thirdly, their number and the consistency of their testimony; fourthly, the conformity of their testimony with experience; and fifthly, the coincidence of their testimony with collateral circumstances."[1]

Now let us test the witnesses (Peter, Matthew, Paul, John, etc.). *Honesty:* These disciples suffered for the resurrection. They were persecuted and imprisoned because they taught the resurrection. Do you think they would suffer for something they knew to be a lie? Note their candor in relating things to their own discredit. Matthew tells of Peter's denial of Christ (Matt. 26:69-75). He also tells of the apostles' ambition to be first in the kingdom (Matt. 20:20-28). John tells of their failure to understand (John 20:9). This obviously shows their honesty in dealing with one another. If they were dishonest these things would not have been recorded.

The things that cause men to lie cannot be found among these witnesses. *Fear:* If this would have caused them to lie, they would have denied the resurrection. Even in the face of threat they still testified. *Greed:* There was nothing to gain as far as greed would be concerned by testifying of the resurrection. They suffered for their testimony. *Ambition:* No power was gained by claiming they had seen the Lord; hence, they didn't lie. These men were honest.

Competence: This refers to their ability to secure information and know whereof they speak. They certainly had the opportunity. They had been with Christ since His baptism (Acts 1:21-22). They were certainly mentally competent. Matthew was a tax collector which required profound knowledge of both Hebrew and Roman law. Luke was a physican. John had the ability to note details (John 20:7). These were not ignorant men.

Number: The testimony of two is better than one and three better than two. You finally get to the point that you need no further witness (Luke 22:71). Over 500 claimed they saw the Lord (1 Cor. 15:6). They all would testify to the same. We conclude from this test that these indeed are true witnesses, thus what they said about seeing the resurrected Christ must be so.

Appearances

1. **When Jesus appeared after his resurrection, it proved he had been raised.** Let's take Thomas as an example of how his appearance was convincing that he had indeed risen

---

[1] Ferrell Jenkins, *Introduction To Christian Evidences* (Guardian of Truth Foundation, Fairmount, 1981) p. 136.

from the dead. The other disciples told Thomas they had seen the Lord. Yet he said, "Except I shall see in his hands the print of the nails, and put my finger into the print of the nails, and thrust my hand into his side, I will not believe" (John 20:25). When Jesus came to him, He said, "Reach hither thy finger, and behold my hands; and reach hither thy hand, and thrust it into my side: and be not faithless, but believing" (v. 27). Thomas' answer was, "My Lord and my God" (v. 28). His appearance was convincing that this was the resurrected Lord.

2. **Jesus appeared to many.** When Jesus appeared to His disciples and others, they could tell that indeed this was the man that had been put to death. His appearances were "**1.** To Mary Magalene (Jn. 20:14-18; Mk. 16:9 first). This was obviously her second trip to the tomb. **2.** Two other of the women as they returned from the sepulchre. This was after the angel told them of the resurrection (Mt. 28:9). **3.** To Simon (Cephas) (Lk. 24:34; 1 Cor. 15:5). **4.** To the two (Cleophas and another) on the way to Emmaus (Lk. 24:13; Mk. 16:12). **5.** To the eleven and 'them that were with them' (Lk. 24:33, 36-49; Mk. 16:14; Jn. 20:19-23). This was on the evening of the first day. Thomas was absent. This seems to be the same as 'the twelve' of 1 Cor. 15:5 (cf. Jno. 20:24, for a similar usage—an official usage). **6.** To above 500 brethren at once (1 Cor. 15:6). **7.** To James (1 Cor. 15:7). **8.** To 'all the apostles' (1 Cor. 15:7) after eight days, with Thomas present (Jno. 20:26-29). **9.** To Peter, Thomas, Nathanael, the sons of Zebedee, and two others at the Sea of Tiberias (Jn. 21:1-14). This was the third appearance to the disciples (v. 14). The two previous appearances would be 5 and 8. **10.** To the eleven; the giving of the 'Great Commission' in Galilee (Mt. 28:16-20; Mk. 16:15-18). **11.** To the eleven at Jerusalem (Lk. 24:44-49; Acts 1:3-8). **12.** To the eleven on the Mount of Olives near Bethany (Lk. 24:50-53; Acts 1:9-11). The ascension. **13.** Last of all of Paul (1 Cor. 15:8; Acts 9:1-9)."[2]

Conversion of Saul

1. **This argument was presented by Lord George Lyttelton in 1747.** "Like so many of the literary men of his time, George Lyttelton and his friend Gilbert West were led at first to reject the Christian religion."[3] "Fully persuaded that the Bible was an imposture, they were determined to expose the cheat. Lord Lyttelton chose the Conversion of Paul and

The risen Jesus appeared to:

Mary Magdalene at the tomb

Two other women

Simon

Cleophas and another man on the way to Emmaus

The eleven and them that were with them

Above 500 brethren at once

James

All the apostles (including Thomas)

Peter, Thomas, Nathanael, the sons of Zebedee, and two others at the Sea of Tiberias

The eleven in Galilee

The eleven at Jerusalem

The eleven on the Mount of Olives

Paul

[2] Ferrell Jenkins, *op. cit.,* pp. 138-139.

[3] Lord Lyttelton, "Observation on the Conversion and Apostleship of St. Paul." *Evidence Quarterly,* Vol. I (No. 2, 1960), p. 29. (This work is analyzed and condensed by J. L. Campbell, D.D. Cambridge, Mass.)

The **conversion of Paul** was of itself a demonstration sufficient to **prove** Christianity to be a **divine revelation**.

Mr. West the Resurrection of Christ for the subject of hostile criticism. Both set down to their respective task full of prejudice; but the result of their separate attempts was, that they were both converted by their efforts to overthrow the truth of Christianity."[4] Lyttelton said, "The conversion was of itself a demonstration sufficient to prove Christianity to be a divine revelation."[5]

Lyttelton lays down four propositions which he considers to exhaust all the possibilities in the case. "1. Either Paul was 'an *impostor* who said what he knew to be false, with an intent to deceive; or 2. He was an *enthusiast* who imposed on himself by the force of 'an overheated imagination'; or 3. He was '*deceived* by the fraud of others;' or, finally, 4. What he declared to be the cause of his conversion *did all really happen;* 'and, therefore the Christian religion is a divine revelation.'"[6]

2. **Paul was not an impostor.** Men who so act do so because of a motive. There was no motive to cause Paul to lie about seeing the Lord. What could have caused the man to change? *Money?* Wealth could not have been the motive, for that was on the side that he left. Poverty was on the side that he had taken. He has now identified himself with those would sell their possessions that they might give to the poor (Acts 4:31-37). *Reputation?* No, that was on the side forsaken as well. He is now united with a group that is held in world contempt. The leader of this group had been put to death among criminals. "On the other hand, the wisest and the greatest men in all the land indignantly rejected the teachings of this sect."[7] Hence, he had nothing to gain as far as a reputation; rather he lost any that he might have had. *Power?* No, that too was on the other side. He certainly gained no place of prominence or power. Rather he considered himself not worthy to be an apostle (1 Cor. 15:9-10) and as the chief of sinners (1 Tim. 1:15). In writing to the Corinthians he rebuked some for claiming they were of Paul (1 Cor. 1:13). He merely considered himself as a "fellow-laborer" in the kingdom of God. *Pious fraud?* "Had he fabricated the story of his conversion he would have located it in a place so remote or hidden that there could be no witnesses to refute. Instead of that the miracle Paul's conversion, with its great light from heaven exceeding the brightness of the sun, is placed in the public highway near Damascus; at noonday, when their senses could not

---

[4] Lyttelton, *op. cit.*, p. 29
[5] Ferrell Jenkins, *op. cit.*, p. 142.
[6] Lyttelton, *op. cit.*, p. 30.
[7] Lyttelton, *op. cit.*, p. 31.

be deceived, and when all the accompanying soldiers and commissioners were with him on the spot."[8] The miracles that Paul performed were done openly, thus showing that his conversion was not a matter of fraud (Acts 13:4-12; 14:8-ff; 16:16-18). Paul had no motive for becoming an impostor.

3. **Paul was not an enthusiast.** None of the marks of an enthusiast can be found in Paul. *Temper:* He was always governed by reason. His zeal became a servant to him rather than his master. *Melancholy:* "This is the mark of misguided zeal, but it is never found in Paul; he is always rejoicing, never brooding (Col. 1:24; Phil. 4:4-7, etc.)."[9] *Ignorance:* Paul was a man of "much learning" (Acts 26:24), having set at the feet of Gamaliel. *Vanity or self-conceit:* "Vanity and fanaticism usually go together. Men of this type flatter themselves that on account of their superior worth they are the recipients of extraordinary favors and gifts from God, and of these they make their boast."[10] Many passages speak for themselves as to Paul's modesty and humility. It was neither Paul that planted, nor Apollos that watered, but God who gave the increase (1 Cor. 3:4-7). He meekly said it is "not I, but the grace of God that was in me" (1 Cor. 15:10).

Paul could not possibly have been swept away with enthusiasm. An enthusiast always sees what they are looking for; yet Paul was looking for anything but Christ. "In the circumstances a wild enthusiast might indeed imagine he saw a vision, but it would be one urging him onward to do the thing he had started out to accomplish. With nothing having happened to change his opinion or alter the bent of his mind, it would be as impossible for him, in a moment, to have imagined the complete revolution that is recorded in the New Testament as it would be for a rapid river to 'carry a boat against the current of its own stream.' We might add, as well expect the mightly rushing river itself, without any cause to stop in its course and rush violently backward up a steep mountain side, as to expect the whole current of Paul's thought and feeling and imagination and purpose to be instantly reversed without any cause. It could not take place."[11]

We need not lose sight of the fact that he had witnesses with him that saw the light (Acts 22:26). It would be equally impossible for them to become carried away and imagine they saw a light and heard a voice.

Having seen that Paul was not an **impostor**, not an **enthusiast** and was not **deceived** by others, we must conclude that Paul really did see **Jesus alive** on the road to Damascus.

8 Lyttelton, *op. cit.*, p. 32
9 Jenkins, *op. cit.*, p. 143.
10 Lyttelton, *op. cit.*, p. 34.
11 Lyttelton, *op. cit.*, p. 35.

4. **Paul was not deceived by others.** This third possible solution can be dismissed very easily. It would have been *impossible* for the disciples to produce a light brighter than the noon-day sun. Neither could they cause him to hear a voice speaking out of the light. Nor could they cause him to be blind for three days and then return his sight. There were no Christians around when this took place.

5. **It really did happen.** Having seen that Paul was not an impostor, not an enthusiast and was not deceived by others, we must conclude as George Lyttelton did, that Paul really did see Jesus alive on the road to Damascus. Hence Jesus has been raised from the dead.

For these reasons we believe that Jesus was raised from the dead.

Questions

1. How is the resurrection of Christ the "hub" of the gospel? _____
   _____
   _____

2. What is the "Swoon Theory" and how would you respond to it? _____
   _____
   _____

3. How do we know that the disciples didn't take the body? _____
   _____
   _____

4. How do we know that the enemies didn't take the body? _____
   _____
   _____

5. What prophecy was fulfilled when Jesus was raised? _____
   _____
   _____

6. What change did the disciples make and how does that prove the resurrection of Christ?
   _____
   _____

7. What change did the Jews make and how does that prove the resurrection of Christ?
   _____
   _____

8. List the criteria for a credible witness. _____
   _____
   _____
   _____

9. How would you prove that the apostles were credible witnesses? _____
_____
_____

10. How does the conversion of Saul prove the resurrection? _____
_____
_____

11. What was Lord George Lyttelton's argument about the conversion of Saul? _____
_____
_____

CPSIA information can be obtained
at www.ICGtesting.com
Printed in the USA
FFOW05n0758060914